A THEORY
OF CITIZENSHIP

A THEORY OF CITIZENSHIP

■   ■   ■

Organizing Plurality in Contemporary Democracies

Herman van Gunsteren

Westview Press
A Subsidiary of Perseus Books, L.L.C.

Copyright © 1998 by Westview Press, A Subsidiary of Perseus Books, L.L.C.

Published in 1998 in the United States of America by Westview Press, 5500 Central Avenue, Boulder, Colorado 80301-2877, and in the United Kingdom by Westview Press, 12 Hid's Copse Road, Cumnor Hill, Oxford OX2 9JJ

Library of Congress Cataloging-in-Publication Data
Gunsteren, Herman R. van.
   A theory of citizenship : organizing plurality in contemporary democracies / Herman van Gunsteren.
      p. cm.
   Includes bibliographical references and index.
   ISBN 0-8133-6862-6 (hardcover). — ISBN 0-8133-6863-4 (pbk.)
   1. Citizenship.   2. Democracy.   3. World politics—1989–
I. Title.
JF801.G86   1998
323.6'094'091717—dc21   98-9738
                                                                                          CIP

The paper used in this publication meets the requirements of the American National Standard for Permanence of Paper for Printed Library Materials Z39.48-1984.

10   9   8   7   6   5   4   3   2   1

867917

Contents

v

□   □   □

Preface

The revolutions of 1989 inaugurated a period of constitutional politics and of transformations in regime that continues to this day. The political order of nation-states and East-West power blocs is gone, but we cannot yet discern the stable shape of a new order. This order is still in the making; and the form it eventually takes, for all we know, might well depend on contingencies and on the actions of citizens as much as on broad trends.

I therefore invite readers of this book to consider with me the place of citizens in the transformations under way: What notion of citizenship is appropriate in current circumstances, and what orientation can citizens give to ongoing constitutional changes? Our goal in this consideration will not be to detail the day-to-day world of politics in all its glory and squalor. Instead, we will seek to define a principle, an attitude, that could make a difference in that world. While exploring the conditions that stimulate citizenship, we will focus primarily on how the practical exercise of citizenship—even under conditions that are far from ideal—keeps it alive. In the book's first two chapters, I have outlined the politics and meaning of citizenship in various epochs. In the next four chapters, we will inquire into what contemporary citizens actually can do, especially in the turmoil of post-1989 democracies, to organize their differences. These first six chapters, in essence, focus on the practice of freedom. In the last five chapters, we will concentrate on the process of emancipation—on what it takes to become a free citizen—in part, through institutions of education, immigration, and socialization. Together, these chapters present a coherent vision of citizens as organizers of a pluralist polity, a theory of citizenship for contemporary democracies. I hope that my readers will be stimulated by this vision to contribute more actively as citizens to the constitution and ongoing evolution of a republican order in their own states and communities.

I wish to thank a number of colleagues who commented on my earlier attempts to get the subject right: the late Aaron Wildavsky, Hans Oversloot, Martin Rein, Geraint Parry, Mavis Maclean, Etienne Balibar, Robert van der Veen, Paul den Hoed, Sasja Tempelman, Thyl Gheyselinck, Arie de Ruyter, Alfred Pijpers, Margo Trappenburg, Koen Koch, Grahame Lock, Mark Bovens, Lolle Nauta, Claus Offe, Jos de Beus, Paul 't Hart, and Désanne van Brederode. I received fine editorial assistance from Phia Koppers. I am fortunate to have found in Westview Press not only a publisher but also people I soon felt I could trust. I am particularly grateful to Rebecca Ritke, copy editor, for her delicate and clear suggestions. I am grateful to the Dutch Scientific Council for Government Policy for making it possible to commission studies of "citizenship practices," some results of which appear in Chapter 7. While working as a Council member, I profited from the interventions of fellow members and from cooperation with Paul den Hoed, Raoul Wirtz, Anne Paret, and Edith van Ruyven. Ideas in the chapter on plurality were first developed in collaboration with Sasja Tempelman. I thank Mary Douglas for a conversation in which she explained things I wish I had understood when I started studying citizenship. We never wrote that article on "The voice of the citizen in hierarchies," but some of the ideas for it can, I hope, be found in this book.

Herman van Gunsteren

Part One

□   □   □

Why Citizenship?

ONE

□　□　□

Citizenship on
the Political Agenda

POLITICAL EARTHQUAKES AFTER 1989

The year 1989 marked the beginning of a period of political surprises—of things we thought could not happen that nevertheless did. Events again and again took place that were not only unexpected and unlikely but also theoretically impossible—at least, no provision had been made for them in political theory current at the time.

Who in 1985 could have imagined Václav Havel as president of the Czech republic, or Nelson Mandela leading South Africa? Who could have predicted the worldwide resonance their rise to power would evoke? The nonviolent accession to office of these erstwhile political prisoners marked an unprecedented reconquest of public space from totalizing systems and the bureaucratic and military servants of those systems. The public actions and statements of Havel and Mandela, which have remained remarkably free from resentment and revenge, have underscored the nature of the conquest: The two leaders have continued to insist on dialogue and cooperation with their cocitizens, although the latter group includes the former oppressors of the citizenry. The new leaders willingly engage in labor-intensive political craftsmanship and reject temptations to circumvent the process by force or threat of violence.

These exemplary citizens who now occupy the foremost offices of their republics do not stand alone, of course. They are members of broader movements of people who refused to collaborate, who said "no" to systems that supposedly guaranteed the conditions of their existence. These new citizens likewise rejected the sort of violent contestation that characterized earlier revolutions. It is worth remembering that "velvet" revolutions were possible because people acted as citizens, in whatever situations they found themselves—whether in the ranks of the opposition or among those in power. A number of soldiers, politicians, and civil servants stood shoulder to shoulder with ordinary people in the streets, risking their positions in order to achieve freedom for all in the republic. The Berlin wall was brought down by similar cooperation among antagonists: dissidents, power holders, and ordinary people alike.

Unprecedented shifts in political power take place not only under autocratic or totalitarian regimes but also where change is regularly effected by democratic procedures: The political parties that controlled Japan and Italy after World War II have been unmasked as corrupt and incompetent, and unseated. For the first time in the history of its party government, The Netherlands is ruled by a coalition that does not include the Christian parties of the center. Everywhere, voters and dissident politicians are demanding change—no mere changing of the guard, but a completely different style of conducting politics. Rulers are showing sensitivity to such demands but are finding it difficult to devise appropriate responses. Only the regents of the European Union appear immune to the infectious spread of popular refusals to go on with politics as usual. The outdated attitudes of those long accustomed to the isolation of high office could cost them, as well as their constituents, dearly—or so think many ordinary citizens.

Frustration among citizens with what they perceive as unresponsive leadership is on the rise, and citizens' refusals to go on with politics as usual do not always flow through democratic channels. Extremism of the far right, marginalization of strangers and other "superfluous" people, disgust with politics, and indifference to new poverty in old welfare states have given rise to illegal and often violent acts. In addition, international mobility and communication make the maintenance of law on the territory of the state increasingly difficult. The national society is no longer the self-evident context for political action and order. Other contexts are often more important, not only for firms but also for national authorities themselves. Both increasingly model their policies after "unavoidable" international realities. They cooperate with other states but at the same time engage in regime competition with them. States try to distinguish themselves, to develop an exclusive profile of taxation, business opportunity, and style of living, with a view toward making themselves attractive to footloose firms.

Changes can be detected also in political representations of reality. The pyramid model, based on the logic of rational and central rule, is passé (Toulmin 1992; Van Gunsteren 1976). Sovereignty is divided and fragmented, and it, too, has become an outdated concept. Nowadays, people must deal with multiple and shifting nodes in their relations with entities that formerly were represented by a single center. Politics and rule-making take place in diverse locations that are no longer connected to each other in a stable, hierarchical order. Where people have begun to notice and to accept these developments, the former centers increasingly are losing their grip.

More and more people sense that the tectonic plates on which their political acts are based are shifting. The constitution, within the constraints of which politics normally is conducted, has itself become vulnerable to politics. In various countries, new constitutions are being written and enacted. The content of constitutions and the rulings of constitutional courts once again matter, and they might even be decisive during tense, life-and-death political situations. In periods of "normal" politics, the political actors are known, limited, and anchored in professionalism; however, in periods of constitutional or revolutionary politics, as in France after 1789 or in Eastern Europe two centuries later, this is not so (Ackerman 1991). Political outsiders and amateurs suddenly find themselves in situations in which they turn out to be crucial actors, and established politicians and parties suddenly are deprived of their assumedly normal powers.

Such times are fascinating but also full of risks. The orientation that normal politics previously provided (even as it gave rise to popular boredom and disgust) is no longer fully reliable or valid, and thus people are much more "nakedly" dependent on each other. When institutional definitions of what counts as political reality are no longer taken as self-evident cultural facts (like a common language, or driving on the right-hand side of the street), people are forced to provide meaning, orientation, and dependable relations among themselves. There is no fixed set of institutions that reproduces a self-evident "we" to do this for them. In such uncertain situations, some search for security in the givens of race, nation, religion, or international commerce: These types of communities offer a limited but often temporarily workable "we." Others reject all such totalizations and seek salvation in the strictly individualistic pursuits of consumption, self-rescue, and enjoyment of life as it comes. A third way is that of citizenship—that is, the individual's acceptance and deliberate molding of a public community of shared fate.

Citizens are connected by the ways in which they govern themselves and agree to be governed, by the organization of their conflicts and differences. It is precisely in turbulent periods of constitutional change that citizenship is put to the test. Where old institutions are crumbling, a robust notion of citizenship may provide an alternate site or a new set of building blocks for reconstructing the republic under changing circumstances. In a time of transition, a valid and vital conceptualization of citizenship may help to keep political contestation within acceptable limits. Citizenship offers a compass for orientation and reorientation in new and unfamiliar situations. It does not guarantee success—corruption, intimidation, and the infliction of physical harm and other forms of injustice remain characteristic of a time of transition—but it is a welcome help in setting out a common course for people who feel the political ground shifting under their feet. In a period of political earthquakes, people's interest in a practical and workable theory of citizenship naturally increases: We know that we need a notion of citizenship sufficiently grounded in the current political reality to engage the support of a majority of citizens. Today, the theory of citizenship begs for reconsideration in the light of post-1989 events and developments. Such was my goal in writing this book.

CITIZENSHIP AS A DYNAMIC PRINCIPLE OF CONSTITUTIONAL POLITICS

The events of 1989 and their aftermath have catapulted the world into a period of constitution making and transformation of political regimes that transcends the logic of the nation-state. In the deliberations that have accompanied the drafting of new constitutions, the elementary problems of living together in a late or postmodern setting have been addressed: How should political decisionmaking be organized so as to facilitate meaningful individual living, productive business practice, ecological responsibility, and justice for future generations? These are the great questions at stake in North America, Europe, South Africa, and around the world—in all the more mundane debates and fights in which the location and legitimation of political decisionmaking are being reconsidered. To be sure, nation-states are still playing a prominent role in this process. For instance, the intergovernmental conference that was to formulate a revised constitution for the European Union in 1997 was run by civil servants handpicked by the governments of nation-states, rather than by delegates to a constitutional convention elected by the people. But nation-states are no longer the uncontested central actors in the constitution-making process; nor are they obvious forums in which the results of the process will necessarily be implemented and modified.

Many people feel that we live in a transitional period in which new political entities will continue to develop alongside and in competition with the previously dominant nation-state. Although few believe that the nation-state will soon disappear altogether, many are convinced that its status is fundamentally changing from dominant form of political organization to one form among many. Externally, the nation-state is related to and in competition with political entities such as the European Union, the World Trade Organization, the North Atlantic Treaty Organization, multinational firms, and entities that are as yet unnamed, or are illegal, and thus are not formally recognized as political regimes (for example, mafia organizations). Internally, powerful mass media, big money, and the consumer society in recent times have fundamentally altered the traditional landscape of parliamentary democracy, political parties, and the rule of law within which the position of the citizen as voter and addressee of the nation-state was once secured. Nowadays, the differences between government and opposition, and therefore the significance of elections, are often unclear. Elections are supposed to confer legitimate political power, but how can they do so when there is no choice to speak of? Increasingly, people ignore the messages that governments send because they seem of little relevance to daily life.

Now that many political issues and actors are situated outside the framework of the nation-state, which moreover has altered its ways of operating, the question of support for the prevailing political regimes in nation-states becomes crucial. On what grounds can they claim legitimacy? In liberal political cultures, these regimes are legitimated by individual consent. However, when elections in nation-states with parliamentary parties are no longer the primary and obvious avenue for registering consent or dissent by citizens, citizenship itself becomes a problematic constitutional issue: In what venue, then, is political consent legitimately to be registered? At stake are the status and meaning of citizenship itself, as well as the definitions of who may or may not be a citizen. A measure of the new constitutions will be their capacity for defining and guaranteeing the position of the citizen—their citizen-producing capacity. Citizenship is a principle of constitutional reconstruction, in the sense that citizens should play an active role in it as well as in the sense that the constitution should foster citizenship.

When the constitution of a political regime fosters citizenship as a dynamic principle of its organization—when a regime is "owned" by its citizens—we call that regime a *republic*. Citizens of a republic are both rulers and ruled: They rule directly, or ultimately, and they obey fellow citizens in their ruling authority as officeholders. A republic is local. A world-level approach to establishing constitutional regimes by such methods as adopting and enforcing human rights charters lacks local depth and vitality. For the time being, human rights protections need firm anchoring in the local political regime in order to be effective.

I use the term "republic" to forestall identification of this political regime with the nation-state and its parties, parliament, and welfare arrangements. Every democracy based on a parliamentary system is a republic, but not every republic is a democracy based on a parliamentary system. A republic is a political regime in which those living under it have some real say but not necessarily through parliamentary party governance. Whether consent can be organized and registered by other routes is an open question. The matter cannot be decided beforehand by theoretical fiat. To limit citizens' choice to either parliamentary party democracy or dictatorship is to exclude many other options. If the European parliament and European parties do not get off the ground, it does not necessarily follow that we should give up all hope of making the European Union a regime that is in some meaningful sense governed by its citizens. That is not to say that other options can easily be realized. How to organize government by "the many" has been a central problem from the beginning of political theorizing. For such a government to be viable, it had to be tempered or mixed, according to Aristotle, and to be kept in line through civic virtue, according to many later thinkers. In modern times, theorists have insisted that democracy must be tempered by basic, individual rights, lest it become "totalitarian democracy." If the risks of democratic degeneration are real, then new checks will have to be invented for those situations of governance that do not permit a direct application of the checks that emerged historically in the form of parliamentary party democracy.

ON THE AGENDA OF REDEMOCRATIZATION

Over the past fifteen years, citizenship has reemerged as a priority on the political agenda of many established democracies, which have felt the need to "redemocratize." In Great Britain this is evident in the movement for a written constitution and in the Conservative government's "citizens' charter," in which the citizen is conceived of as a consumer who exercises rights vis-à-vis service organizations. In the United States, Newt Gingrich and his Republican party's Contract for America immediately come to mind; however, many other, less central and visible groups have insisted with equal firmness on citizen rights and have criticized their violation by public authorities with equal vigor. Some groups advocate citizen trials, citizen police and militias, citizen schools, and citizens bearing their own arms. "The search for those who blew up the federal building in Oklahoma City has taken us into a netherworld of militants who believe that the federal government is all one plot against their liberty" wrote Gary Wills (1995:50–55). Wills asserted that such groups offer not only actions but also arguments, "an internally consistent case for the illegitimacy of federal acts."

> But there is something new about the groups coming to light after Oklahoma City. However those groups differ among themselves—some espousing violence, some not; some religious, some secular; some millennial, some pragmatic—they all agree in their intense fear of the government, and they have framed a complex analysis of the machinery of governmental repression, one that even non-extremists share on this point or that. In fact, it is hard to trace the exact line where extremism spills over into "mainstream" concerns about liberty.

France recently has witnessed seemingly contradictory developments: a right-wing rejection of foreigners on French soil, combined with government demands that French citizenship be exclusive of other citizenships and be acquired through explicit choice rather than quasi-automatically; large demonstrations of youth against this official separation between "them" and "us"; and individuals' refusals to comply with uniform dress codes in French schools (the head scarf worn by some Islamic girls has been a particular focus of contention).

Political leaders in The Netherlands have repeatedly criticized the "calculating citizen" who uses state welfare arrangements to his own advantage, at the same time as they worry about an alleged gap between themselves and ordinary citizens, who seem more and more disaffected and disengaged from politics. In Germany, this theme has been echoed by descriptions of *Parteiverdrossenheit* (popular antagonism toward political parties). The German consensus has been ravaged since reunification by complaints that the arrogant West Germans have been treating the *Ossis*, or East Germans, as second-class citizens who cannot be trusted because of their former "collaboration" with the regime of the Deutsche Demokratische Republik (DDR). The question of granting German citizenship to foreign workers who have lived in Germany for a period of determinate length also has been controversial, both in theory and in practice, as gangs set fire to foreign workers' dwellings.

In Italy, when judicial magistrates some years ago began to expose the corrupt political establishment, their actions were welcomed by many ordinary citizens who felt that such an initiative was long overdue. The arrests and indictments effectively started a broader movement of constitutional reform that continues today. A guiding concern in these reforms is to find novel ways to bridge the gap between political elites and ordinary citizens.

The fostering of feelings of European citizenship and the development of some citizen rights has been on the agenda of the European Union for years. Resistance in various countries against the Maastricht treaties, and especially against the clauses on citizen rights, has made European citizenship a contested issue on national political agendas. This, in turn, has fueled the revival of national(istic) notions of citizenship.

The problems of citizenship take various forms on the political agendas of contemporary democracies, but their new visibility suggests a common link: Political issues increasingly are being addressed in terms of citizenship. A general similarity also is evident in the policy areas and concerns involved—immigration, poverty, and discrimination; corruption and inefficiency in the provision of public services; the gap between politics and ordinary citizens; and the gap between national and supranational identities. In the debates referred to earlier, these issues are most often discussed in terms of who is in and who is out—in terms of loyalty, belonging, and sameness—with the implicit notion of citizenship being that of unity and consensus. Such terms, however, do not fit well with the increasing differentiation and pluralization evident in post-1989 politics. Would it not be more effective to develop a vision of citizenship that acknowledges contemporary differences and focuses on the creative, positive task of citizenship—organizing those differences—rather than on the negative imposition of unity through uniformity?

The success of technological, capitalist societies in the post-1989 era in resolving contemporary political problems will depend to a large extent on their political resilience and their decisionmaking capacity. The latter, in turn, will depend on the vitality of civil society, which itself is determined by the activities of citizens. If we as citizens do not succeed in achieving a democracy befitting our times, more will be lost than we can begin to imagine. Let us proceed then, to seek a better understanding of who we are as citizens and of what we are groping toward.

TWO

□ □ □

Theories of Citizenship, Old and New

Citizenship is not an eternal essence but a cultural artifact. It is what people make of it. Like language, it depends on, and changes with, usage: Changes in political regimes and agendas usually entail changes in the uses and meanings of citizenship. To understand the potential of citizenship, what it is and what it could become, we must know its history and understand what it meant to people before us.

This chapter maps the coordinates of meaning within which contemporary notions of the citizen are situated. It then briefly traces the development of thinking about citizenship in liberal democracies since World War II. Following this, the strengths and weaknesses of the three varieties of citizenship theory that predominated during that period—liberal, communitarian, and republican—are assessed. Their weaknesses, I submit, have become liabilities in post-1989 social and political conditions: These theories no longer provide sufficient orientation, because the social conditions they presuppose no longer obtain. Out of selected elements of the three earlier theories, I then develop an alternative idea that promises to provide a better orientation for citizens in our time: neorepublican citizenship.

A FIELD OF MEANINGS

In a republic, the power of the sword and all other functions of authority are exercised by cocitizens. Thus, a citizen is both ruler and ruled. In order to fulfill this double function of ruling and being ruled, citizens must have a minimum of autonomy, judgment, and loyalty. On this point theoreticians by and large agree. When these three aspects of citizenship are fleshed out, however, differences of opinion emerge. Who is autonomous? Is anyone ever really autonomous? Is complete independence required, or is the mere absence of slave-like relations sufficient? Is a person without property—who, economically speaking, has no say—autonomous? Does a hermit who never participates qualify as a citizen? And an addict who "chooses" to continue his addiction and thereby actually loses his freedom to choose and to lead a different life? What standards and categories of judgment are sufficient for the exercise of citizenship? Should one know the name of a cabinet minister or be able to recognize a mass murderer? What mistakes of judgment disqualify a person as a citizen? Should the voices of persons suffering from dementia be heeded? To whom or what should citizens be loyal: their nation, future generations, former generations, newcomers, settled "illegals" (illegal status surely does not deprive individuals of all human rights), the law, the authorities, the republic, or the queen?

The substantive elaborations of each of these three aspects of citizenship—autonomy, judgment, and loyalty—thus show considerable diversity. Moreover, ideas about the interactions and interdependence of these three qualities also differ. Can someone who has no capacity whatsoever for judgment be called autonomous? Should one count the voices of citizens who, in exercising their autonomy, allow themselves to be misled by others, and who as a result are obviously exercising faulty judgment? Can there be any autonomy without loyalty? And depending on how one answers this last question, might requirements of loyalty be imposed on citizens who work for the news media?

The diverse possible understandings of the qualities of citizenship further multiply when we add to these variations two more distinctions: those between citizenship in a strict and in a wide sense, and citizenship in a formal and in a substantive sense. The term citizenship is used in a strict sense to refer to the status of political equality and participation, and in a wider sense to refer to status and participation in the wider social sphere. The term is used in a formal sense to refer to a legal status with rights and duties, and in a substantive sense to refer to the real disposition and political influence that persons have or lack.

When Dutch cabinet ministers recently lamented a lack of "civic responsibility," they were speaking as citizens in a strict, political sense, about citizens in a wide, social sense. Their critics, who were invoking the elementary right of the citizen to say "no" and to remain uninterested, based their interventions on the formal, legal definition of citizenship. Questions about the education of new citizens take on a similar ambiguity as they are batted back and forth in this field of diverse meanings. Is our goal in educating newcomers their achievement of political citizenship alone, or should we also require their introduction to local habits, norms, and values? Can loyalty be expected from people who actually have no say in the affairs of society and thus are excluded from citizenship in a substantive sense? May a formal requirement of knowledge of the official local language be imposed when access to courses in that language is nonexistent? How should we regard political refugees who have been formally admitted to citizenship but for whom there is no substantive and livable place in society?

The multiple meanings of citizenship are givens that cannot be erased by a simple legal or scientific definition. Even if it were possible, such an intervention by experts would not be accepted automatically, because more is at stake here than conventions and formal relations. The different meanings that people attach to citizenship have both material and moral consequences and are often rooted in their convictions about justice. However, an awareness of the diversity of the field of meanings and of the positions that are taken up within it might help to avoid quarrels and confusion. Clarity is not achieved by ignoring the existence of an ambiguous field of meanings. Those who attempt to assert such "clarity" in fact are creating further ambiguity and misunderstanding. Progress toward clarity may be expected only when with due respect for the views of others, one takes up a clearly marked position within the field of meanings of citizenship. The position presented in this book is that of neorepublican citizenship. Before one can explore and defend this position, one must understand the intellectual context in which it is anchored—that is, the competing theories of citizenship that emerged in liberal democracies after World War II.

THE DEVELOPMENT OF A CITIZENSHIP DOCTRINE

A number of valuable studies on aspects and periods of the history of thinking about citizenship have been published in recent years (Heater 1990, Roche 1992, Oldfield 1990, De Haan 1993, Kymlicka and Norman 1994). This section provides but a brief sketch of recent doctrinal developments, as a background against which the neorepublican position presented in this book can be appreciated.

Between 1945 and 1980, the ruling consensus in Western countries, following the work of T. H. Marshall (1950), ran roughly as follows. Citizenship has three aspects, namely, that citizens have a say in political decisionmaking; access to courts of law that are manned by cocitizens who judge according to rules that equally apply to all citizens; and a guarantee of minimum socioeconomic conditions of existence. Citizenship is a matter of emancipation, of successively realizing these three aspects of political, legal, and socioeconomic participation for all people who find themselves on the territory of the state. Given this vision, citizenship ceased to be practically and theoretically interesting once it had been acquired by almost everyone, because it had lost its distinguishing qualities. Further development of the three constitutive aspects of citizenship—the political, the legal, and the socioeconomic—took place under the headings of "democracy," the "rule of law," and "the welfare state." These principles were applied not only within the sphere of the nation-state but also beyond it—for instance in firms and transnational arrangements—with the goal of achieving justice for all human beings. Gradually, as the concept of citizenship became so all-encompassing, it lost virtually all significance.

This situation began to change toward the end of the 1970s. Rulers started speaking of democracy, the courts, and the welfare systems as overloaded by the demands of citizens. Firms began demanding freedom from the yoke of bureaucracy so as to concentrate once again on their mission of making a profit. The idea that the liberal-democratic welfare state had burst out of its supporting structures soon was a commonplace. But how could it be brought back within manageable limits? Institutions and consensus had been based on assumptions of continuing economic growth and a parallel increase in rights and social protection. Would it help if individual citizens behaved differently? Not as mere holders of rights and receivers of care, but as responsible individuals who chose from among various options in the marketplace and then accepted the consequences of those choices; or as mutually connected people who gave each other a helping hand; or as proud members of a public community, for the sake of which they were prepared to make sacrifices? These three different theoretical conceptions of citizenship—the liberal-individualist, the communitarian, and the republican—were further elaborated in confrontation with one another. Instead of How do you get it? the question of citizenship had become What is it? Competition between the different schools of thought for the "best" notion of citizenship brought an enrichment and sharpening of insights. Notwithstanding their differences, however, all were based on the assumption that there can be such a thing as a single conception of citizenship that is most fitting and most just in all circumstances. By the 1990s, this assumption ceased to be self-evident because the political context within which citizenship was supposed to do its work had changed considerably.

At present, after long periods of stagnation or stability, political relations and alignments within states are again in flux. The nation-state itself is no longer the self-evident center of the exercise of power and the creation of order. The contours of nation-states have become blurred in an international system that is multipolar and is unpredictably changing. Steering by national governments on the basis of data concerning their societies has become increasingly unreliable. It is now clear to everyone that governments cannot control national societies. The free movements of people, goods, and money across frontiers are too numerous and too massive. In this context, citizenship has become plural—it is no longer exceptional that one person be a citizen of several different communities—for example, the European Union, Turkey, and Amsterdam. There is a plurality also of appropriate conceptions of citizenship—one being preferred in one situation, and the other elsewhere—as the primary purpose of notions of citizenship is no longer to make people more equal but to enable them to organize plurality (in other words, to cope peacefully with bothersome or surprising differences between themselves and others with whom they cannot avoid dealing).

The themes of debates about citizenship have shifted as well: More attention now is focused on situational judgment than on the essentials of citizenship, and the old emphasis on rights is now accompanied by an emphasis on institutional duties, concerns, and loyalties. In other words, the point of departure for analysis is no longer unity but the multiple identities of minorities who have a responsibility to live together as citizens in one republic. The authoritative representation of "fact" by scientifically ordered data and of "will" by constitutionally anchored democracy has been overtaken by a diversity of media that present only the aspects of social reality that they can profit by portraying. Increasing attention is being paid to local and situational factors. This is remarkable in a world that is becoming more and more international and unified. Could it be that precisely because more and more people now palpably experience the unity of the world, the value of local and bodily proximity and uniqueness are at last receiving due recognition in the theory and practice of politics? A key question is whether this acknowledgment of the importance of the local will be expressed in terms of a nationality, race, religion, or another exclusive principle for grouping people, or alternatively, in more inclusive terms of common citizenship.

But why prefer citizenship? For an answer, let us return to the 1980s and to the question of why, precisely at that time, citizenship rose high on the political agenda. This was a period of individualization, or more precisely, of dehierarchization. In a hierarchy, everything and everyone has a proper position, which is stably related to other positions. During the 1980s, hierarchies became disestablished not only in the imagination, as in the 1960s, but also in their actual ordering and disciplining capacities. Individuals increasingly lost their fixed positions within hierarchical political orders. Many became disinterested fatalists or calculating individuals who turned to politics and heeded its requirements and laws only when it paid them to do so. Others vested their primary public commitment in religious sects, idealistic movements, or interest groups. Although those reactions are quite different, the one focusing on the individual and the other on voluntary groups, nevertheless both have turned their backs on the crumbling hierarchy of politics. For them, politics has lost its primacy as a principle of order. As a consequence, political authorities who try to reestablish a hierarchical order by appealing to morality, community, the nation, and renewed discipline meet with very limited success. Many addressees simply do not listen; and among those who do, quite a few experience such appeals as empty rhetoric referring to an order that no longer exists. Painting that order in harmonious colors doesn't make it less of a lie.

Given the glaring inadequacy of those reactions to dehierarchization, the attractiveness of citizenship as an ordering principle increases. It accepts both the reality and value of individualization and the necessity of cohesion by taking the individual citizen as the paramount principle of public order. From this starting point, other institutions in the hierarchy can be salvaged and connections with interest groups, sects, and calculating or disinterested individuals can be reconstituted. This book develops this theme of the voice of the citizen in hierarchies. The citizen is the axis from which cohesion and community can form and be reformed. Hierarchy is no longer given, nor can it be centrally produced. Citizens themselves must act so as to produce it. Formerly, individuals were more firmly embedded in the totality of tradition or of disciplining systems that were handled by experts. Now, without any given totality, they have to rely more on each other. The awareness that such is indeed our precarious but exhilarating situation is beginning to dawn on both rulers and ruled.

This, however, is but one side of the picture. The other is that just as with hierarchy, citizenship itself is not given. It is no deus ex machina, coming out of the blue to save the republic. Citizenship is itself a public institution that needs not only personal enthusiasm but also other institutions in order to function. This institutional support for citizenship will be given due attention in the chapters that follow. There is a danger in such a focus, however. Studies and policies that pay ample attention to supporting institutions and preconditions have tended to make active citizenship disappear from view by treating it as a dependent variable. This book stresses the crucial independent role of citizenship in the transformation of political regimes. But it conceives of active citizenship as an institution that can only work as part of a network of institutions. What has changed over the past twenty years or so is the place of citizenship in such networks, which has become more central and decisive than it used to be.

THREE THEORIES OF CITIZENSHIP

Liberalism, communitarianism, and republicanism, the three varieties of citizenship theory that have been most prominent in recent decades, have been amply analyzed in professional journals and books. Their strengths and weaknesses therefore will be recalled only briefly here. We need this background sketch in order to show that since 1989, their strengths have become less relevant and their weaknesses more of a drawback. The new political and social realities have made the older theories of citizenship obsolete, because the kind of social order that they presuppose no longer obtains. Political and social realities have outgrown the framework within which these three theories of citizenship were embedded.

In liberal-individualist theories, the citizen is represented as a calculating holder of preferences and rights. The utilitarian variant of such theories is based on the axiom that individuals maximize their own benefit: That is, they calculate what choice of action will render the highest product of the value attributed to the desired situation multiplied by the probability that this situation will occur ($C = V \times P$, or choice is equal to value times probability). In the "individual rights" variant of liberal-individualist theories, choice is defined by citizens' calculations of their own rights within the limits of their respect for the rights of others. To the individual, this structure of rights is given. The rights themselves may or may not be derived from utilitarian considerations by the lawmaker. It is important to note that both variants accept individuals, with their rights, opinions, and choices, as givens, and that both variants explain and justify politics in terms of nonpolitical givens. Citizenship and other political institutions are means that are accepted only conditionally—that is, as long as they, in the individual's calculations, foster the maximization of private benefit.

There are two main problems with such a view of citizenship. First, how can individuals be prevented from destroying each other and from destroying the basis of their mutually beneficial interaction? The war of all against all, the "tragedy of the commons," the receivers of unemployment benefits who secretly work—these all illustrate the same problem. The problem is individualism; it is not that people are evil or malevolent. People also can destroy each other through friendliness. For example, imagine a burning theater with a single exit, and everybody saying, "After you."

The second problem has to do with the ways in which individuals and their ideas are formed. The insights and preferences of autonomous individuals might originate from "impure" processes: The information they were provided might be biased or meaningless, or their preferences might have arisen from a fit of anger. Should individual ideas and preferences be accepted as sacrosanct, even if it is clear that the holders of these preferences would have rejected them, had they realized how they came about? And isn't the conceptual ideal of a fully autonomous individual whose preferences and insights are immune from contingent outside circumstances internally inconsistent? After all, individuals who remain disconnected from all contingencies are nothing. They cannot, in fact, have any preferences at all (except by chance, on which they are forbidden to depend). Yet, is not the ideal of an individual's being entirely determined by contingent circumstances similarly inconsistent? Such a person is not an individual, but a plaything of whatever happens.

These problems were not so urgent as long as individuals still behaved "responsibly"—as long as they went to the polls and did not vote for antidemocratic parties, or as long as they refrained from collecting health or disability insurance payments when they were not truly ill or incapacitated. Those days, however, are over. Many people no longer go to the polls, and antidemocratic parties obtain votes. People work without paying taxes. They pretend to be ill or unemployed, and collect benefits while continuing to earn money on the side. They dodge efforts to distinguish welfare cheaters from "rightful" claimants by hiding behind protections of privacy.

The remedies that have been suggested for these problems have not proven effective—at least, not as long as they were conceived within the framework of liberal-individualist theories of citizenship. All have centered around the cultures that support democracy. The viability of democracies, it is said, depends upon such matters as civic-mindedness, religion, education in democratic rules, or the development of a public morality. If citizens completely lack these attributes, democracy cannot exist. However, if these attributes are embraced too intensely, democracy might also be destroyed. In the first case, democracy would perish from egoism; in the latter, from fanaticism. The challenge is to avoid those extremes and maintain a happy medium. However, even if true, these insights cannot constitute a remedy for the problems of individualistic citizenship. It is important to see why.

Civic-mindedness will hardly develop through individualistic people urging each other on. Civic-mindedness, legitimacy, and public support arise as by-products of other activities and events. We prevent their coming about precisely by directing our will, intention, or manipulation toward them. The will is contrary to the nature of the desired result, as is the case with the wish to fall asleep or the desire to be spontaneous.

De Tocqueville showed how strictness in religion kept individuals in American democracy within reasonable limits of freedom. Sharing his insight that religion and democracy counterbalance each other, however, makes little practical difference. A nonbeliever cannot be converted on the grounds that his conversion would be conducive to democratic peace between individuals. One cannot become a true believer through calculation.

Dahl (1956) claimed that consensus on basic norms is necessary in order to make a democracy work. Such consensus needs to be reproduced through education. But in a society of calculating individualists and lacking such a consensus, who will educate the educators? Education is no remedy, if qualified educators who share Dahl's basic consensus cannot be found.

An appeal to public morality also will not help, in a society of pure individualists. The development of such a morality will continue to stagnate as long as we try to deduce it from a variety of private moralities (Van Gunsteren 1991), for two reasons. Firstly, when private moralities conflict, which one should publicly prevail? Or should we make do with the overlapping consensus between them, even when this consensus remains silent about the real and unavoidable ethical choices that holders of public office have to make? Secondly, holders of public office may (be obliged to) do things (for instance, use force) that persons in their private capacity are forbidden to do, or that are not allowed by any of the prevailing private moralities. It is precisely to keep such actions completely out of the private sphere that they are entrusted to public offices and regulated by public laws and adversarial procedures. The rules and moral requirements associated with exclusively public actions cannot be derived from exclusively private moralities—at least, not directly.

These efforts to circumvent the weaknesses of liberal-individualist theories of citizenship cannot succeed. On the one hand, rational calculation provides insufficient motivation to accept the proposed repairs. The rational insight that it is better to be a believer doesn't make one so. On the other hand, an acceptance of the given historical fact of belonging to a moral or religious community, or an acknowledgment of the nonderivative character of public morality, constitutes an exact denial of the individualist, nonhistorical, and nonpolitical premises of liberal-individualist theories. This does not repair their weaknesses but simply contradicts their core convictions. Such denials are in fact varieties of communitarian or republican theories of citizenship.

Communitarian theories of citizenship strongly emphasize the fact that being a citizen involves belonging to a historically developed community. Whatever individuality the citizen has is derived from and circumscribed by the community. In this vision, the citizen acts responsibly when he stays within the limits of what is acceptable to the community. Loyalty and education in loyalty enable both the community and its individual members to flourish.

There is much to be said for this conception. Firstly, it avoids the problems of liberal-individualist citizenship that were pointed out earlier. Individuals are formed by the community. By sticking to the acquired codes of conduct, they will ensure the continued existence of the community and avoid mutual destruction. They simply repeat the successful formula that enabled the community to originate and survive. Deviation from the code is regarded as corruption and must be resisted. A community in decline can be saved by fighting corruption and returning to its origins, its beginnings. In this way, authority and the successful formula may be restored.

A second reason for advocating communitarian theories of citizenship lies in the insight that identity and stability of character cannot be realized without the support of a community of friends and peers. A person with a strong character is steadfast in changing circumstances and is not easily knocked off balance. For most of us, however, such constancy depends upon the continued existence of, and our membership in, a community of friends who more or less think and act as we do and who share our ways of life. Time and again, research and historical experience have shown that people systematically underestimate this dependence (Nussbaum 1986; Douglas 1987; Sandel 1982; Milgram 1974). Individual autonomy and independent judgment are not what they appear to be. They are dependent upon the same community against which they may be in revolt. This dependence often remains hidden behind a naive self-image. Individualists who have lost such naivety and who acknowledge this dependence will cherish and seek to maintain the community that preserves their individuality. However, they often fail in this because to them, the community is a means. This fact contradicts the alleged essence of a community: its existence as a "natural" and valuable context of action and judgment, a context that is valued for its own sake. A community that is merely a means is not a community.

The foregoing already has touched upon objections to communitarian theories of citizenship. The first objection is that insight does not lead to change but rather prevents it: Seeing that belonging "naturally" to a given community is vital for citizenship does not help when such a community is not available. What is "natural" is simply there or not there; it cannot be fabricated. In modern societies, communities cannot be taken for granted and for that reason, are seldom "natural." There is a plurality of communities and of individual combinations of memberships. In such a society, the conscious creation and cultivation of a community that can be taken for granted is an internally contradictory activity.

A second objection to the communitarian perspective is less concerned with how realistic it is than with how desirable it is. Communities are notorious for imposing restrictions on freedom. Emancipation often has been achieved through liberation from the compelling and unfair ties of a community. The emphasis on "right thinking," which easily emerges in communities that cultivate their own existence, is petrifying. The modern state is supposed to protect its citizens against such dangers. It limits and regulates the reach of communities and protects individuals against them. Given this task, communitarian policies of state governments are suspect for more than one reason: Not only are such policies likely to violate the state's neutrality as to the variety of communities—existing or emerging, tightly integrated or loose, religious or territorial—but by embracing the communitarian perspective, the state also risks neglecting its function of protecting citizens against the stranglehold of communities.

The insight that individuality, autonomy, and judgment cannot exist without a common basis does not necessarily entail acceptance of the communitarian perspective. Communities are both indispensable and dangerous. The state should not be identified with the communities it regulates. The state allows room for the existence and creation of communities and tempers their excesses. Yet what is it that enables the state to do so? What communality offers the context for doing this? One answer is: the public community, the republic.

Republican theories of citizenship can thus be seen as a particular variety of communitarian thinking. They place a single community, the public community, at the center of political life. Courage, devotion, military discipline, and statesmanship are the republican virtues. Individuality can appear, and individuals can mark their place in history by serving the public community. This is where individuals find fulfillment and (possibly) public happiness (for the use of this term, see Arendt 1965:124).

The objections against the classical republican conception of citizenship are obvious. In politics, military virtue is dangerous stuff that is better kept at a distance. This conception does not pay enough attention to economics and trade, nor to the softer aspects and fulfillments of private life. Republican virtues are unilaterally masculine. The republican perspective makes one community absolute and shows too little appreciation for the characteristic values and diversity of other communities.

Classical republicanism clearly is too far out of step with the times to qualify as a compass for contemporary citizens. It may arouse curiosity or admiration, but it lacks practical bite. It does not necessarily follow, however, that classical republicanism is to be rejected out of hand. It can serve as an inspiration for ongoing efforts, such as that by Philip Pettit (1997), to rethink and rebuild the republican idea as an alternative to currently popular forms of liberalism, communitarianism, and populism. This book is part of that movement. Further on, I present a thoroughly revised version of republicanism that promises to do better as a guiding value in the ongoing reconstructions of democracies.

OLD THEORIES IN CONTEMPORARY SOCIETY

The three theories of citizenship—liberal, communitarian, and republican—are unsatisfactory and offer too little guidance. This is so because the societal conditions they presuppose no longer obtain and cannot be restored simply by insisting on the value of those theories. Social relationships and processes largely develop beyond the frameworks of social reality presupposed by the older perspectives. The theories no longer match today's society.

Contemporary society is not a "civil society" of autonomous individuals. Complex organizations and accumulations of capital to a large extent determine the course of events. Individuals, especially those at the top, are usually not heroes, but well-disciplined managers, trained through therapy or other means to act like adults, guided by a well-understood intertwining of personal gain and the benefit of the organization or department they work for. Instead of friendships, they have networks of relationships.

In this society of organizations we find an overwhelming variety of "communities," some of which remain in existence longer than others. Beside the familiar communities of nationality, religion, and business and labor, we now find a host of less familiar and less established ties that often play an important role in the lives of individuals but that we cannot easily call communities. In this society, government bodies, too, have lost their established places. The national state has become but one center of authority amidst a shifting field containing many others.

The proliferation of communities and governing bodies in the society of organizations has its consequences. A first consequence is that political and social identities have become less stable and more varied. Individuals—the substrata of citizens—are bouquets. They compose their own mixed identities out of various connections and bonds. These individuals are not the natural bearers of civic-mindedness and civic virtue, nor are they naturally inclined (however often this may be claimed) to calculate all action in terms of their own wealth and power. Modern individuals' preferences, perceptions, and ways of "calculating" vary and are no longer directly and compellingly derived from the established ties of work, family, and the state. The articulation and aggregation of the supposed wishes and needs of citizens by established intermediary organizations that fit these traditional bonds often fail to represent the individuality, the self-composed bouquet, of today's citizen.

A second implication of the proliferation of governments and communities is the disappearance of a relatively homogeneous middle class, previously considered the backbone of a stable republic of citizens. This class consisted of those not rich enough to buy the support of others and not poor enough to have to sell their vote, of those who had a vested interest in the continued existence of a republican order. Until recently, this class was made up of paid employees and independent businessmen, and the members of households that lived on their incomes. Individualization has dissolved the unity of those households. With the rise of postmodern lifestyles and postindustrial production processes and organizations, the old middle class is a dwindling minority that is rapidly losing its attractiveness to new recruits.

A third consequence of the developments described above concerns government steering. Public planning today is even more difficult than it used to be. From the point of view of those governing it, society is becoming less well known. The categories in which social realities are represented (by numbers and diagrams) are gradually losing their efficacy as descriptors of increasingly complex social actualities and processes. They do provide snapshots, but these pictures often divert decisionmakers from the right track. The insight that rulers need new categories and coordinates seems to be widespread. Yet when they have to specify what those categories should be, rulers are tongue-tied or can only talk at cross purposes, and thus, fail to reach a new consensus. They struggle on with the old categories and coordinates and find their bearings as best as they can, without conviction or commitment, with all kinds of "pictures" retouched ad hoc. This, surely, cannot seriously be described as planning. Such steering is rather to be characterized as "thriving on chaos" (Peters 1988). Contemporary society, which from the point of view of its governors is insufficiently known, may rightly be called The Unknown Society.

In this contemporary society, matters are determined neither by established communities nor by predictably calculating individuals, nor by militarily virtuous servants of the republic alone. All these are present, but they play a variable role amidst a changing range of other actors. None of the three theories of citizenship that were discussed earlier fits with contemporary society as (far as) we know it. The kinds of motivations and social relations these theories presuppose do not obtain. Those who cherish those theories thus are tempted to reverse this dictum and say that society does not fit with what they value, with their theory, and should therefore be changed. By moralization, by selective interpretation (excluding what does not fit their basic assumptions), and by social engineering, they will try to reform society in such a way that citizenship, such as they conceive of and value it, will flourish. From a moral point of view, such a practice is questionable. It takes the voices of citizens seriously only when they say the right things. When they "misbehave," they are to be brought into line through education and conditioning. Apart from being questionable on moral grounds, a policy that is aimed at changing society in order to reestablish the social conditions of earlier times also is not viable. Efforts to radically turn the tide of the postmodern developments that form the air and water in which contemporary citizens live simply cannot succeed.

None of the three conceptions of citizenship can be realized in contemporary society. Shall we then dismiss citizenship as an outdated and unattainable ideal? Must we then engage in constitutional politics without citizenship as a dynamic principle? Such a conclusion would be premature. It is true that none of the three conceptions can be realized; but we can use some of their elements to fabricate a theory of citizenship that makes sense in our time. Call it fabrication, synthesis or bricolage—we have to work with what is at hand, with the institutions and ways of thinking and acting that have evolved. My conception of neorepublican citizenship is the product of this bricolage. This conception does not require that we change social realities before it can begin to work its changes. It accepts the facts of contemporary plurality and of the insufficiently understood but nevertheless operative social realities that we have labeled The Unknown Society. It conceives of working in and on those realities—of the organization of plurality—as the primary task of contemporary citizens.

NEOREPUBLICAN CITIZENSHIP

The neorepublican conception of citizenship includes elements of communitarian, republican, and liberal-individualist thinking.

First, let us consider a few communitarian elements: The citizen is a member of a public community, the republic. For the citizen, this community occupies a central position. Yet from the point of view of the individual—the person who among other things, is a citizen—this community is but one among many, albeit a community with a special position. In that respect, it is similar to the National Bank in The Netherlands, which is a bank among others but has a special position and task—that of guarding the structure that enables all other banks to properly carry out their activities. By analogy, the task of the public community is to guard the structure that enables other communities to develop and to expand their activities. A core task of the republic is the organization of plurality, not only of individuals but also of communities. The hallmark of the republic resides in the way it interferes with other communities. Although for practical reasons such interference may be directly effectuated, in the first and last instance it is mediated and legitimized by citizens. The republic creates and protects the freedom of individuals to form communities, to join them, and to exit from them.

The neorepublican theory of citizenship also contains republican elements. It knows virtues, but they are not the traditional military ones. They concern more peaceful public service through debate, reasonableness, tolerance of plurality, and carefully limited use of violence. The term virtue implies that more is needed than simply abiding by the rules. It is a matter of sensibly, competently, and responsibly dealing with authority, and with situations and positions of dependence. These functions cannot be exhaustively laid down in rules. Individual competence also is essential for the exercise of citizenship. A chairman who does not break the rules but is otherwise incompetent in presiding over and guiding a meeting can be a disaster.

The emphasis on competence should not be exaggerated. Virtue stands not only for competence, but also for an ethic of civility, of decent behavior. Neorepublicanism acknowledges an autonomous ethic of the public domain that is not purely derived from private ethics or opinions, but is rooted in the public domain itself. Because individuals in their functions as citizens are of central importance in the public domain, such private ethics and opinions do play a role, but never more than a mediating, indirect one. Citizens' contributions are more than the mere sum of the opinions and desires they have as private individuals.

What is the position of the individual in the neorepublican theory of citizenship? Citizenship is conceived of as an office in the public community. This means that a citizen is not to be identified with the so-called ordinary person, nor with the entire person. It also means that there are conditions for admission to the practice of citizenship. The republic should not only facilitate access but also formulate and maintain those conditions. It does not merely wait for individuals to present themselves spontaneously as citizens but also promotes the development of people into independent and competent citizens. Individuals are not naturally given; they are socially formed. The republic does not simply leave the "reproduction" of citizens to existing communities, but verifies whether the social education offered by those communities actually allows for admission to citizenship. Where this is not the case, or where people lack the formative support of the community, the government interferes.

In the republic, citizenship is the primary office: Office holders are primarily citizens who hold an office as part of their exercise of citizenship. They may, at times, do things, or have things done, that "normal" citizens are not entitled to. Yet, the existence of these special powers should not support the misunderstanding that such holders of offices cease to be citizens as soon as they accept or fulfill their office. Precisely because these offices are so susceptible to abuse, we want them to be held by, and under the supervision of, our cocitizens. The task of reproducing citizens is at issue in every government action.

We can more systematically explain the elements of neorepublican citizenship by reference to three concepts: *the public realm, organizing plurality,* and *action.*

The term "republican" situates citizenship squarely in the *public realm.* It is a matter of public institutions and public ethics. Citizenship is conceived of as an office, an institution, in the republic. Every citizen has a right to exercise this office, and when doing so, his authority is no different from that of other citizens. They are equal in their political standing and say. Political equality is a requirement of citizenship. Social equality—that is, the elimination of differences of standing and power in the social sphere—is not required. However, citizenship in a republic does demand that inequal social relations not be allowed to prevent any individual from having reasonable chances of access to political equality.

I have used the term "neorepublican" to signify that unlike older republican convictions, this type of citizenship demands no overarching or total claims of allegiance to the republic. Neorepublicanism acknowledges that individuals may have deep differences and deep loyalties to other communities. It does not require that people always put loyalty to the republic above those other loyalties. But it does require that in situations where people have to deal with their differences, they do so as citizens—that is, in such a way that access to a position of political equality remains a real option for all persons involved. This brings us to the organization of plurality, the second set of elements that characterize neorepublican citizenship.

To *organize plurality* is the primary task of neorepublican citizens; being able to do this competently is their primary virtue. *Plurality* here refers to differences among people who share a community of fate. These differences may be of various kinds—pleasantly surprising and exciting, annoying or outright threatening, disturbing and incomprehensible; personal, cultural, or physical. The point is that people are so situated with regard to each other that they cannot avoid dealing with their differences. (Ignoring or avoiding them, then, is to choose one particular way of dealing with differences; and it is interpreted as a choice for which citizens can be called to account.) When individuals are so situated that they cannot avoid bumping into each other without giving up their ways of life and work, when they have to deal somehow with their differences, we speak of a "community of fate." A community of fate is a given, in the sense that people find themselves involved in it without much forethought or choice, and in the sense that they cannot extricate themselves from it without paying a heavy price. However, what individuals do with this given, how they interpret and transform it, is their choice and responsibility. They can kill the disturbing other, or put him in a concentration camp. They can exploit or humiliate, go into hiding or flee. They can join in religious ecstasy or charitable activities, love or compassion. What citizens are required to do with a community of fate in which they find themselves is quite special: They must interpret and transform given relations between people in such a way that firstly, such relations are worthy to be chosen (willed) by all those involved, and secondly, so that each individual acquires a position of political equality from which his actual voice can be raised and his choice be revealed. The duty of citizens is to transform a community of fate into a republic that can be willed by all who are involved as citizens.

In order to achieve this, people need competence, a repertoire of moves and skills. Goodwill and a consensus on norms and values, which have a central place in many discourses on "feelings" of citizenship, are not enough. They are neither a necessary nor a sufficient condition for transforming a community of fate into a republic of citizens. Of course, tolerance and respect—the wish not to humiliate and not to be humiliated—are important; but without competence—the ability, inventiveness, and good judgment—to actually organize differences, they come to naught. The competence of citizens is never a purely individual matter, because the matching of competences among all those involved is important. Obviously, it is preferable that all U.S. citizens communicate in broken English than that they speak their own individual mother tongues perfectly. It takes two to tango. Citizen competence also does not imply individual perfection: All that is required is the willingness and human ability to begin changing given relations between people—a community of fate—in the direction of citizenship for all. What is required is that citizens act so as to (re)produce citizenship. This brings us to the third set of elements that characterize neorepublican citizenship.

Citizenship is created and recreated by citizens *in action*. While many theories focus on the conditions and limits of citizenship, neorepublicanism concentrates on the actual situated exercise of citizenship. Of course, conditions are important, but they are not constitutive of citizenship: The existence of the right conditions does not guarantee the successful exercise of citizenship; nor does their absence prevent citizens from acting in exemplary fashion, as did some Dutch citizens under the surely imperfect conditions of German occupation during World War II. The most important condition of citizenship, one could say, is its actual exercise. As with competence, here also, elitist perfection is out of the question. What counts is that in the actual situation in which they find themselves, in which conditions are never ideal, imperfect citizens get going on the road toward citizenship for all in the republic by dealing with their real differences. What counts most, then, is not the arrival at a final destination, but movement, and the direction in which it takes place. What is decisive is whether people act in such a way as to create and foster citizenship.

All public action, undertaken in whatever special public office in the republic, may be evaluated from this point of view. Neorepublicanism thus presents a conception of citizenship that is narrower than most others—in that its goal is political equality—but that is nonetheless applied more widely—that is, to all public activities. Outside the public sphere, neorepublicanism is more hesitant to intervene than are many other conceptions. It calls for interference only when private relations are such as to prevent reasonable access to citizenship.

In the neorepublican view, social consensus is not a condition for successful citizen activity. Plurality, a lack of consensus, is the characteristic situation in and on which citizens have to work. When they are successful in organizing their differences, the result may be called consensus. Consensus is the outcome that their action is aimed at. It does not make sense to make consensus a condition that must be met before persons can begin to act as citizens. Putting consensus before citizen action is putting the cart before the horse.

The same logic applies to freedom: Full freedom is not a condition for citizen action. Citizen action, rather, concerns people who are on the road somewhere between slavery and freedom. When they move in the right direction, when they address actual problems of unfreedom, freedom may appear in their actions as a kind of by-product. Freedom is not a possession or a condition, but rather, a quality of action that may reveal itself in the doing.

When citizens act repeatedly with some measure of success in transforming disruptive differences into livable relations, their actions may generate, reinforce, or transform a public culture—that is, a repertoire of established ways of dealing with conflicts, both actual and potential, and a shared definition of acceptable results. Ultimately, acceptability has to be evaluated from the standpoint of justice. However, in imperfect situations, imperfect citizens have to be content with, or to make do with, less than full justice; with avoiding violence and humiliation; with small steps in the direction of citizenship for all. The web of relations that results from repeated citizen action and that we call political culture is a highly desirable by-product of citizen action. When it fails to materialize, citizen action will wither. A supportive political culture is like oxygen for citizens; but it is oxygen that they, like plants, produce through their own activities. Such a political culture cannot be fabricated through moralizing or social engineering. It can only be fostered and cherished after it is established, and it can only be furthered by using its institutions and convictions to deal with actual differences among citizens.

Such are the main elements of neorepublican citizenship, which I have worked out and put to the test in the remainder of this book. Of course, this notion is not entirely new. It builds on earlier theories of citizenship: on Aristotle's idea of ruling and being ruled, on Rousseau's ideal of the citizen who obeys no one but himself, on T. H. Marshall's conceptualization of the political, juridical, and socioeconomic aspects of citizenship, and on Benjamin Barber's vision of politics itself as the activity of creating whatever common standards of justice we have.

Indirectly, the theory of neorepublican citizenship also draws on the work of Arendt, Douglas, Habermas, Foucault, and Wittgenstein. It follows Hannah Arendt in her notions of power (as arising out of acting together) and acting (as beginning something new and as showing who you are in a web of relations), as well as in her insistence that politics should not be centered around work and social life. However, I do not agree with Arendt that politics should be restricted to the public realm and its concerns. Although the public realm is the natural home of politics, I believe that politicians and citizens should move into other spheres of life in order to secure a reasonable possibility of access to politics for all citizens.

My views echo those of Mary Douglas in her insistence on the importance of institutions. Thinking, perception, and valuation, as Douglas has shown, are shot through with institutionally defined notions of right social relations. This holds true for those like us, in liberal cultures, who have been taught to believe and act "independently" as individuals. Like other varieties of culture, individualism is a culture dependent on supportive institutions. These institutions have been the more successful if they have induced us to perceive individual autonomy as something "natural" and to forget our dependence on them. Upon reflection, however, we realize that citizenship is not a natural attribute of individuals but an office in the set of institutions that we call a republic. The voice of the citizen needs an order of institutions, a hierarchy, both to sound and to have effect.

Jürgen Habermas, to me, is a shining example of what it takes to hold onto the ideals of the Enlightenment and the French revolution at a time when harsh differences and postmodernism have made them questionable. He does not presuppose rationality as a kind of axiom, nor does he give up on it. Rationality, for him, is "in the making," something both found and created by participants in social and political processes, rather than guaranteed by history, as in Hegel.

Michel Foucault has played an important part in undermining the once self-evident Enlightenment truths, but he is closer to Habermas than one might think. In an interview the year he died, he said: "I am interested in what Habermas is doing. I know that he does not agree with what I say—I am a little more in agreement with him—but there is always something which causes me a problem. . . . The problem is not of trying to dissolve them [relations of power] in the utopia of a perfectly transparent communication, but to give one's self the rules of law, the techniques of management, and also the ethics, the ethos, the practice of self, which would allow these games of power to be played with a minimum of domination" (Foucault 1988:18). Late in life, Foucault added to his earlier studies of truth-games, discipline, and power relations a genuine interest in the practices of freedom. This is worked out in interviews and in volumes 2 and 3 of his *Histoire de la sexualité*. At the beginning of the interview already quoted, he said: "Liberation opens up new relationships of power, which have to be controlled by practices of liberty. . . . Yes, for what is morality, if not the practice of liberty, the deliberate practice of liberty?" (Foucault 1988:4) This study's focus on competence in the organization of plurality continues that line of thinking.

My emphasis on the actual exercise of citizenship rather than on its preconditions is inspired by Ludwig Wittgenstein, who insisted that concepts not be abstracted but that they be studied as parts of ongoing practices, or "forms of life." Wittgenstein did not deny that people have things in common, but insisted that those common elements can be fully appreciated only if they are studied in their various situated appearances and uses. Following this line of reasoning, citizenship is to be studied locally. In this book, a number of specific local examples from my own country, The Netherlands, are offered, as well as examples from a number of other countries and regions. These will only be illuminating to the reader who is willing to think along with them by adding his own similar or contrasting experiences. If the reader can recognize the family resemblances in these various local strands, then a more general understanding of citizenship will have been gained.

Part Two

□   □   □

What Citizens Do

THREE

□   □   □

Plurality in
The Unknown Society

What do citizens actually do? Like all other people, they eat, sleep, and pursue their private affairs. But where do they reveal themselves as citizens, and by what actions? Formerly, there were three kinds of situations that called for—and thus, defined—citizen action. First, there was normal politics in established democracies, which involved activities like voting in elections, participating in the work of political parties, serving in intermediate social organizations, performing military service, and paying taxes. Second, under dictatorships, there were secret or open activities of resistance and refusal. And third, there were episodes of revolutionary politics that formed transitions to a new order of normal politics and constitutional stability. For a brief period of time, ordinary citizens would be actively involved in relatively unstructured processes of decisionmaking; but after the reestablishment of normal politics, most of them would again leave the political stage to the professional political actors.

Nowadays, we are witness to a fourth, more diffuse, setting for citizen action that combines elements of the other three. Phrases such as "the diffusion of politics" or "the displacement of politics," and "the end of the nation-state" or "the loss of the center," indicate this. Political leaders rise to power by way of normal elections; but in the European Union, they engage in quasi-revolutionary, constitution-making activities that are in fact beyond public democratic control. Citizens may engage themselves against such a benevolent semidictatorship, or they may themselves try to establish a European public space, without envisioning much of a role in it for the European parliament and the so-called European parties. For example, citizens are organizing themselves in environmental movements such as Greenpeace in order to prevent the international transport of nuclear materials, as well as in other movements promoting objectives that transcend national borders. Regional political activities of all kinds are on the rise. Research shows that citizens are active, if one defines their range of activities broadly. But if one sticks to the more traditional notion of politics in the nation-state and looks only at such indicators as party membership, voting turnout, and the like, then citizenship appears to lack vitality.

When people are acting specifically as citizens and when they are not is not easy to determine, these days. With the decentering of politics, boundaries have become blurred. Neorepublicanism offers a degree of clarity by asserting that we see citizens act as such whenever they organize plurality in a community of fate: *That* is what citizens do. But how do they do it? And what is plurality?

We all know that contemporary societies are plural; but in what ways, is not immediately clear. They surely evidence many stubborn differences and catastrophic or pleasant surprises; but we often get stuck when we try to give these a place in established schemes of social order and interpretation. And even when we succeed in doing so, we retain a suspicion that we have missed something important by incorporating them, and that our negligence sooner or later will come home to roost. These are precisely the feelings of people who live in The Unknown Society, or *Die neue Unübersichtlichkeit* (the new inscrutability), as Habermas (1985) called it in his speech to the Spanish parliament. If indeed we live in such a society, then a definition of plurality only in terms of social groups and categories will omit a great many phenomena for which we have not yet established a conceptual category. Therefore, this book—in contradistinction to many other studies, which start at the level of the group—focuses on the micro level of two persons who differ; and their difference is what we shall define as plurality. It is at this level that we situate our conceptualization of how plurality is organized by citizens.

THE VALUE OF PLURALITY

Plurality—differences between people who deal with each other—is what politics is concerned with. Where we find politics, we find plurality. Plurality is, in the words of Hannah Arendt (1959:60), "the condition . . . of all political life," while freedom is its "raison d'être" (Arendt 1968:146). In this view, to practice politics is to process plurality into freedom, to translate "blind," given differences into willed and consciously accepted ones. Plurality is a recurrent theme in political discourse precisely because it is inherent in political life.

In liberal democratic regimes, this theme will always be prominent for the simple reason that the exercise of individual freedom—its core value—tends to generate plurality. This plurality is prima facie legitimate and may be curtailed only in exceptional situations, for special reasons. The burden of proof rests on the curtailer. If you want freedom, you must accept plurality. In liberal democracies, plurality is therefore in principle legitimate, regardless of whether we personally approve of it. This stance is expressed in doctrines of the separation of politics from religion, of law from morality, and of justice from notions of the good.

Plurality may be considered legitimate, but at the same time be disliked or thought undesirable—a price to be paid for freedom. However, in liberal democracies a positive valuation of plurality generally prevails. Why? Firstly, variety and novelty are admired as interesting and worthwhile expressions of creativity. Secondly, plurality is welcomed because it provides a rich menu of choices to individuals who want to change places in society, who want to escape from patterns of living in which they have become entangled. The exercise of the right to live and organize one's life according to one's own insights would become an unbearable burden if one had to start from zero, without being allowed to choose from a menu of available elements. Finally, plurality is valued also because it makes for vitality and resilience. Plurality provides flexibility, facilitates adaptation, and offers the possibility of generating alternatives that may prove indispensable under changed circumstances. Ecological and organizational theories have familiarized us with the idea that diversity and even chaos are essential conditions for evolution and improvement. As Gould (1993:120) wrote:

> If animals were ideally honed, with each part doing one thing perfectly, then evolution would not occur, for nothing could change (without losing vital function in the transition), and life would quickly end as environments altered and organisms did not respond. But rules of structure, deeper than natural selection itself, guarantee that complex features must bristle with multiple possibilities—and evolution wins its required flexibility thanks to messiness, redundancy, and lack of perfect fit. Human creativity is no different, for I think we are dealing with a statement about the very nature of organization—something so general that it must apply to any particular instance. How sad then that we live in a culture almost dedicated to wiping out the leisure of ambiguity and the creative joy of redundancy. . . . Redundancy, and its counterpart of ambiguity in multiple meaning, are our way, our most precious, most human way.

However, even in liberal democracies, not all plurality is valued positively. There are special arrangements for dealing with disturbing or unacceptable manifestations of plurality—for example, rules that forbid discrimination and curtail the exercise of personal freedom when it impinges on the freedom of others. Other examples are the adversarial procedures in law and politics that allow for a period of competition, comparison, criticism, negotiation, and compromise, followed by a decision that is implemented with the backing of the state's monopoly of violence. It is precisely here, in their methods of dealing with disturbing plurality, that liberal democracies recently have been running into trouble. Citizens are contesting or simply ignoring rules and finding clever ways to circumvent them. A crisis of representation has affected adversarial procedures in politics and law, and the implementation of public decisions increasingly bumps into impenetrable walls—areas where public authority ought to exercise its monopoly of violence but that in fact remain impervious to it. Examples are the "no go" areas in large cities, mafia activities, and new communications networks. Liberal principles remain the same, but social reality and the kind of plurality it generates are changing.

THE UNKNOWN SOCIETY

In our discussion, therefore, we cannot ignore the changing social context within which plurality appears and is processed. In today's society, which we may call postmodern, late-modern, or The Unknown Society—the label is of minor importance—plurality has a different place and form than it had in the modern industrial society of the 1950s. The following scheme, which recalls the differences, illustrates this.

MODERN SOCIETIES	THE UNKNOWN SOCIETY
national unitary culture	creolization within global culture
politics of emancipation	"lifestyle" politics
equality	differentiation, difference
organization, hierarchy	reorganization, networks
rationality	rationalities, "we are all natives now"
fixed identity	fleeting and multiple identities
guaranteed representation	problematic, ad hoc representation
the end of ideologies	variety of lifestyles and convictions
pragmatism in politics	fundamentalism in politics

In modern societies, people and their differences could be fairly easily located on a map with coordinates for home, work, education, and religion. Their differences were to a large extent known, and their behavior as voters or consumers could be fairly well predicted once one knew their position on the map. They would by and large behave as did other people in similar positions. Differences were part of an overarching unity of national culture and state policies. The ways in which this unity was subdivided might vary, from pillarization in Dutch consociational democracy to divisions among class lines in France; but the overarching unity, the boundaries of which coincided with those of "the society," was provided by the nation-state.

Nowadays, the nation-state has lost this central, defining role and holds an uncomfortable position between regionalism and internationalization. Many conflicts can no longer be adequately mapped in terms of the division of labor, religious affiliation, and level of education. Even when one knows people's social position in those terms, their behavior remains pretty unpredictable. People often are not what or who they seem to be. They may have multiple or mixed identities, use identities strategically, and change identities or roles at unexpected moments. The established ways of representing this social reality through elections and empirical social research often fail to capture what is going on. Interventions by rulers who have to rely on such representative schemes often misfire. Institutions that earlier helped them to know more and better now often saddle them with institutional ignorance. They do not and cannot know what many others know from direct observation and experience: The Stasi in East Germany in 1989 knew a lot—so much, indeed, that they could not grasp what was going on. Election research has acquired better data and methods, but it is less able now than it was thirty years ago to predict voting behavior.

Rulers react to those deficiencies in various ways. They may ignore them. They may improve the quality of public managers through training and expand the base of managerial experience and knowledge by hiring managers from the business sector. They may try to reform institutions that represent social reality for them—for example, by pursuing other routes of knowledge production (acquiring different advisers); by leaning more heavily on alternative schemes of political representation (e.g., referendums, mass media manipulation, and party reform); or by adopting another style of governing. Or they may try to discipline the social world so that it behaves more in accordance with the established schemes of representation and allows the rulers again to do what they are supposed to do: to govern. All of these reactions have in common that they cannot really surmount the problem of The Unknown Society. On balance, they seem to consist in ad hoc reparations of a paradigm of representative government, which, altogether, make this way of governing quite complicated and unstable. The paradigm is one of analysis and instruction, of knowing better and of designing clever interventions based on this superior knowledge. This paradigm, it seems to me, is no longer tenable. Rulers nowadays have to expect that among the ruled there is always someone who will outsmart them. That is nothing new. What is new and fatal to the older way of ruling is that this unruly behavior is likely to be copied by cocitizens and to become generalized with great speed. It spreads throughout society before rulers know what is going on.

The only viable option for rulers in The Unknown Society, I think, is to accept proliferating and unpredictable plurality and make it an ally. Governing then becomes less a matter of analysis and instruction and more a matter of variety and selection—that is, of accepting variety and coping with it on the basis of selective values. One such value is citizenship. Rulers who let themselves be guided by this value will rely on citizens as organizers of plurality and will evaluate policies and laws according to their citizenship-enhancing qualities.

In present-day society and in its politics, plurality has acquired a different place—a more central and more problematic one. The ways of dealing with plurality and of organizing it, therefore, also should be reviewed. If plurality came in ordered doses, neatly arranging itself under the labels provided by standard schemes of social classification, then we could safely rely on the established ways of dealing with plurality, ways that fit those classificatory schemes and that have been improved on the basis of ample experience and analysis. But when the schemes of social classification themselves seriously misrepresent, or fail altogether to capture, actual plurality, then the established ways of dealing with differences also fall short of their goal. Interventions based on such schemes will unexpectedly misfire. The repertoire that they offer suddenly appears too limited or unsuited to deal with real contemporary plurality. What, then, can be done?

Next to further analysis and adjustment of the existing official repertoire for organizing plurality, I suggest, it is imperative to appreciate and learn about (and from) this disturbing but real plurality that does not exactly fit our schemes. We can study how people, at the micro level of daily life, manage to deal peacefully with potentially disruptive differences. True, in contemporary societies, we find much disruption, violence, and injustice, but they are not rampant. They are shown on television and reported precisely because they are in most places (thank heaven) exceptional. But what about the many cases where violence could have erupted but did not? How do normal people so often manage to maintain peace and relatively civil relations? If we can get a view on how they do this—what skills, ruses, attitudes, and insights it takes—we might subsequently see which parts of this practical but unofficial repertoire are fit to be incorporated into the currently too limited official repertoire for organizing plurality.

Also, once we have an idea of what this unofficial repertoire is, we can inquire why a single act of violence sometimes can make the repertoire disappear into thin air—and change peaceful cohabitation into civil war and chaos. If we understand this, we can try to make the many acts of civility more robust and immune to such interventions. This purpose, in part, has led to the establishment of a number of public institutions safeguarding the legal process, freedom of speech, movement in the streets, and so on. In the new plurality of The Unknown Society, citizens should continue this work of protecting peaceful ways of dealing with difference through the building and revising of public institutions.

CONCEPTUALIZING PLURALITY

Perceptions of plurality often rely on standardizations that depict people primarily as exemplars of a category instead of as individuals making sense out of who they are and what happens to them. From the standpoint of citizenship, this is a fatal mistake. Citizenship is precisely about holding individuals responsible for the categorizations that they use to present themselves and to situate others. And citizen politics is precisely about changing socially established rules of categorization that hinder access to citizenship for all. If we allow our conceptualization of plurality to be dominated by group categorizations as "natural" givens, then a first step away from citizenship has already been taken. Many standard ways of classifying social plurality are thus highly undesirable from the point of view of citizenship. If one goes along with them, then citizenship is already damaged.

For purposes of citizenship, many conceptualizations of plurality start at too high a level—that is, at the level of the group rather than of the individual. They begin by observing that there are different groups and categories of people in society: races, classes, genders, nations, religions, professions, political parties. Thus, plurality is made primarily a matter of relations between groups and among aggregates of people. Subsequently, dealing with plurality in the interaction among individuals is as a matter of fact considered as derivative of these relations.

I think that we should start at a much more basic level—namely, with the experience of plurality of minimally two individuals whose paths in life cross. This plurality is *experienced, constructed,* and *processed* by individuals in their dealings with each other.

Individuals experience the fact that other people are different as a clash, as an opportunity, or simply as a difference. This experience is shot through with construction, with interpretation or with "seeing as" (Wittgenstein 1958:193–208). We see the other person as Chinese, a worker, a general, an artist, and so on. Usually this is a direct perception: We do not first see facts and subsequently look for a matching interpretation to make sense out of them. On the contrary, sense is given *in* experience and perception. We stop at a red traffic light. No reasoning is involved here. A red light means "stop." Our perception and experience are permeated with self-evident (attributed) meaning. The parentheses indicate that although we do attribute meaning, the process is not usually conscious. This point of departure therefore might be called phenomenological.

However, we also consider the social construction of reality, the attribution of meaning, as an activity for which we are responsible, as something that we do. How does this relate to the self-evident character of experience? As follows. We can break through the self-evidence of our experience and of our perception. We can see things in a different light by using different categories and classifications. By creating these new constructions, we can learn to recognize where our first experience also contained interpretation and construction, classification and modeling. Although standard classifications and interpretations are a part of our everyday life experience, they are not obligatory or unavoidable. I experience someone else as a black person or as a general, but the naturalness and compulsion of this experience can be unmasked as a social construction of reality. From these assumptions, it follows that we are coresponsible for the reproduction of self-evident meanings in social interaction.

"Natural" classifications and interpretations serve useful functions. "Normality" provides quick orientation, offers a fund of questions and strategies, and is a focal point around which people arrange their interaction. Normality organizes plurality. Citizenship does not answer the questions of whether and to what extent certain normal interpretations and classifications are useful, but it does set a limit to their use: Citizenship is incompatible with the compulsion of self-evident social classifications when these in fact prevent reasonable access to a position of political equality.

Experienced and constructed plurality is also actively processed by the individuals who are encountering each other. Surprising or disturbing difference is transformed by way of discourse, movements, and procedures; for instance, by saying "I'm sorry"; by going to court; by dancing together and kissing; by being a member of a panel; or by allowing someone to pamper you. Notice that this processing involves more than one person. The other person may speak wise and friendly words, but if I do not understand the language, then our game, our dance, fails. It does indeed take two to tango.

The conceptualization proposed here can be used to understand situations where plurality is at issue. In this vision, plurality is not something that is simply there, it is what individuals construct in their social interaction. Such construction need not be a "blind" process that unfolds behind the participants' backs. Without being able to control it completely from beginning to end, individuals nevertheless influence the direction and outcome of the social construction of plurality in which they participate. As citizens, they are responsible for directing the construction of plurality toward an outcome that instead of simply ignoring or suppressing their real differences, confirms and reasserts the identities of all participants as equal citizens.

Constructing and organizing plurality requires competence and skills that usually are scarce and not equally available to all persons. The degree to which people succeed in directing their constructions of plurality toward citizenship also depends on supportive institutions, as well as on the intensity of the emotions and the nature of the identities at stake—all factors that to some degree exceed the reach of even the best-trained and most rational individuals. If constructing plurality necessarily involves competence, institutions, emotions, and identities, then it cannot be a simple affair; the more so because these four items are both *objects of* and *instruments for* the organization of plurality. Let us take a closer look at them and their complex relations.

Individual Identities

Identities are used to order disturbing and surprising differences. An unknown person becomes "known" by acquiring an identity, a place within existing social schemes. The way in which identities relate to each other is often embedded in the way in which the identities themselves are constructed. The identity of "worker," for instance, relates in contrast to the identity of "capitalist." In the ordering of plurality through the assignment of contrasting or relative identities, various mechanisms of ranking, exclusion, and marginalization of individuals and groups are at work. Take, for instance, the identity of "Jew," and the ways in which it has acquired various places within different systems: as a religious category vis-à-vis Islam or Christianity; as a racial category vis-à-vis (that is, inferior to) the "Aryan" race; and as a cultural category indicating a people of matrilineal (as opposed to patrilineal) descent. All of these labels conceal an "unfair" reduction of plurality.

Although identities are socially attributed, they are also part of our inner experience of self. Our deepest emotions relate to what we believe ourselves to be. This self-awareness uses the social categories with which we have learned to look at others and at ourselves. Thus, we are not capable of freeing ourselves completely from the social dimension, from labeling and attribution in our interaction with others. Our identities are not garments that are draped around an essential and originally naked "inner self" and that we can remove whenever we wish.

However, it does not necessarily follow that individuals have no freedom whatsoever with regard to their self-definition. Under certain circumstances it is possible to resist the social attribution of identity and to go one's own way. But "one's own way" is never a purely personal invention. It is, rather, constructed out of certain patterns that individuals encounter in their culture.

An interesting example is a discussion that flared up some years ago within the Dutch organization of homosexuals, the Center for Culture and Relaxation (Cultuur en Ontspannings Centrum, or COC). Once the vanguard for the homosexual liberation movement, the organization came under attack by homosexuals themselves around 1990. The COC, it was said, pretended to represent "the homosexual." Through its informational activities in schools the organization was said to be confusing young people by telling them what a homosexual "is" and by stimulating them to openly acknowledge their homosexual identity. Children thus would get the impression that they should become an entirely different person, while they did not fully understand what they would be leaving behind by deciding in favor of this metamorphosis. Critics also accused the COC of neglecting the variety of different ways of life into which people might mold their homosexuality. The COC was said to have attempted to ossify homosexuality by presenting it as a definite choice of identity, thereby ignoring that homosexual activity may be a transitory experiment and may be accompanied by heterosexuality. In short, the COC clung to an unambiguous and complete homosexual identity that was no longer accepted by other people who preferred homosexuality. These people refused to be trapped in a specific homosexual identity, opting instead for a more autonomous definition of who and what they were.

Citizenship concerns this refusal, this right to say "no," to move in and out of identities without being trapped in them. In this sense, citizenship occupies a metaposition and is not just one identity amid others. It fulfills a mediating function in the interaction among identities. While questions of citizenship used to be concerned mainly with liberation from serfdom and other legal forms of domination, they now also concern liberation from ossified identities. The emphasis has shifted from the politics of emancipation, in which marginalized groups used their identities as a lever to liberate themselves from established structures (women, homosexuals, Catholics), to lifestyle politics. Individuals refuse to be committed to one identity or to a single, fixed combination of identities.

Although citizenship aims at freedom and rejects slavery in all its forms, it does not foster a limitless diversity of fleeting identities. When developing their own lifestyle, citizens must always take into account that they may be held responsible by cocitizens for the exercise of their citizenship. Citizenship is more than a happy-go-lucky enjoyment of one's own freedom to live as one pleases. It also requires respect for limits that allow one's cocitizens to reveal who they are as well. Those limits forbid every form of social death (Patterson 1982) and humiliation, of treating human beings as if they were nonhuman (Margalit 1996) or cocitizens as if they were noncitizens.

Emotions

Everyone knows that plurality—confrontation with surprising or disturbing differences with other people—arouses emotions. The experience of plurality may involve such emotions as enthusiasm, falling in love, fear, group solidarity against outsiders, aggression, paralysis, surrender, or servility. Such emotions have effects on cognition and on the processing of plurality. Especially when we sense that our identity is at stake, we cannot remain idle. Emotions of fear and anger must be expressed, either outwardly, toward objects or other people, or inwardly, toward ourselves. Fear and related emotions often cause the repertoire of behavior to narrow down to paralysis or aggression; to threats rather than discussion; to the blackening of others' reputations; and to projection of fear onto other people, who become a "danger" by virtue of their difference. Sometimes people, such as drunken drivers, really are a danger. Yet projection may inflate and exaggerate this danger. The danger, moreover, tends to be ascribed to other people who have similar characteristics but in fact are not dangerous at all. Enthusiasm and falling in love, usually seen as positive emotions, may also lead to tunnel vision or blindness, which reduce the chances of sensibly dealing with plurality. However, emotions also can widen the range of actions contemplated. When under pressure and in danger, people often become inventive and disposed to unusual forms of cooperation and compliance. Think of the resistance movements during World War II or of the emotional solidarity that sometimes has arisen between passengers and hijackers.

Democracy, which requires toleration of plurality, has from its beginnings had its shadow side (Sagan 1991). On the one hand, it knew respect for the right of cocitizens to differ; it developed the astonishing idea of a loyal opposition, of antagonistic cooperation, instilled and confirmed through education and legal procedure. On the other hand, it practiced aggression and showed contempt toward outsiders—as revealed in slavery, imperialism, war, and poverty. Democrats felt matters becoming particularly dangerous when these outsiders entered the democratic polity or when the border between the "inside" and the "outside" was no longer clear nor controlled. The way sedentary democracies have dealt with Gypsies is a classic example. In our time, when paranoia has perforated debates on admission to citizenship, on migration, and on social policy, democracy again has become uncertain of itself. This appears in a zigzag treatment of people who are neither inside nor outside the polity. When dealing with such people, who are experienced as "monsters" (because they straddle categories that ought to remain separate), emotions and paranoia surface at inconvenient moments. Today, when people frequently move across borders, it is no longer sufficient to accept and appreciate plurality within the nation-state alone. Citizens must also learn to deal with plurality that exists around the borders of the republic. This entails learning to deal with emotions and emotion-steered practices that come with the experience and processing of this kind of plurality.

Pragmatist theorists of democracy in the period following World War II considered emotions dangerous for politics. In their view, emotions should be kept out of the public sphere and allowed to function only in the artistic and private spheres. They should play no role in politics; or at most, they should play only a censored or controlled role. This pragmatic strategy of control had its drawbacks, however. It stifled the emotion-driven imagination that is required for developing sound policies and viable compromises. Moreover, emotions often made themselves felt along sneaky pathways, of which those involved were unaware—and with disastrous results. In retrospect, it seems wiser to acknowledge emotions and to develop and foster competencies and institutions that allow citizens to deal with them sensibly.

Whether we like it or not, plurality does involve emotions. If we smother or ignore them, they will remain a brute and immutable factor that disturbs political interaction at inconvenient moments. If we recognize them, we can place them in the sequence of experiencing, constructing, and processing of plurality. Thus we can hope to come to terms with emotions and give them a meaningful place in the interactions between a plurality of citizens.

Competence and Institutions

Having considered identity and emotion, the more subjective aspects of the organization of plurality, let us turn to the more objective aspects, those of competence and institutions. Good intentions and a concern with identity and emotions are generally not enough to secure an organization of plurality that is acceptable between citizens. Self-expression alone cannot secure civility. The expression should also be adequate to the situation, be comprehensible to others, and moreover fit together with others' expressive contributions so as to make for a viable way of living together as citizens. This is where competence and institutions come into the picture. Competence refers to good judgment and practical social skills, such as the ability to listen and to express one's position, ideas, and emotions clearly; to exercise self-restraint and self-knowledge; to assess situations; to cope with insecurity and surprises; and to follow the movements and intentions of other people. It also refers to the ability to indicate one's own limits ("If I tolerate this, I will not be able to face myself"); to create a context in which trust and understanding become possible; and to deal judiciously with one's own freedom and that of others.

In practice, competence in dealing with plurality is eminently important. Yet, in theory and in the preparation for practice, it has received relatively little attention. The subject is often avoided because the term "competence" rings bells of elitism and meritocracy. Is not a concern for competence incompatible with equality between citizens and with their autonomy? Are not citizens themselves responsible for deciding what they will do and how well or badly they will do it?

On reflection, however, one cannot fail to appreciate the crucial importance of competence for the exercise of citizenship. Democratization, for instance, goes awry when participants have insufficient skills to hold meetings and lack insight into their pitfalls. And citizens who lack competence in public office will make poor or even disastrous leaders. To practice citizenship requires a minimum of competence. A minimum, not a maximum. Citizens may make mistakes. However, when lack of competence actually becomes destructive, a minimum limit is broken through and intervention takes place. Citizens who lack the required competence are subjected to temporary or longer-lasting restrictions on the independent exercise of their citizenship (for instance, being confined in a psychiatric institution).

Even though the republic, albeit reluctantly, will ultimately interfere with the freedom of citizens in such a way, much is done to prevent matters from getting that far. For instance, schooling and information, subsidies and advice may be offered to citizens who lack certain skills.

When training addresses the citizen's competence, it often does so in two rather unhelpful ways. Either too subjectively—for example, when training becomes psychotherapy—or too normatively, as when it tries to inculcate a consensus on norms and values. Against the first approach, it can be argued that what is required is not psychic balance but social and political skills. (It is true that people who cannot express themselves, or who suffer from severe psychic disorders, cannot act competently as citizens. However, not having those psychic "defects" is surely not a sufficient condition for acting competently.) Against the second approach, it can be argued, as I have done in Chapter 4, that consensus on norms and values is neither necessary nor sufficient for effective organization of plurality between citizens. What kind of competence and training, then, do citizens need?

General rules and theoretical insights play an important part, but in themselves they are not sufficient for acting competently. One has to know which rules apply when; and one has to have the ability to deal with uncertainty, with conflicting values and wishes, and with unique situations. To be able to act competently in this kind of situation requires practical judgment, in which attention to variety and to particulars takes a central place. The competence of the citizen resides in the flexibility with which he can mediate between general rules and insights and special circumstances in such a way as to respect the dynamic and plural nature of the republic.

How can this kind of citizen competence be acquired? Can it, in fact, be learned? For a large number of civic skills, the answer is: certainly, but they are acquired in other ways than by learning the rules and facts by heart. Elements of competence—such as practical judgment concerning the application of rules; the ability to deal with imperfections and one's own failures; and the ability to obtain insight into a situation so that one can act at the right time and in the right way—but also skills, such as competently conducting meetings, require a lot of practice. Citizens do not primarily learn these skills in academic courses on citizenship but rather by being involved in civil practices or institutions. By observing the actions of other citizens and by gaining experience in a variety of practices, the citizen builds up a repertoire of examples, insights, and actions.

The repertoire is built up not only from citizens' actual personal experience but also from seeing others act and from hearing stories. A responsibility forum, which always involves storytelling, constitutes a most important learning place for citizen competence. There, storytelling, experience, and reflection are intertwined. When a citizen is called to account in front of a judge, for instance, the way in which his hearing or trial is conducted may teach him something about competent and responsible acting. Acting, evaluating that acting, and learning how to act are brought together in a "hall of mirrors," in which the different parts are reflected in each other (Schön 1987:220).

One must remember, however, that reaching perfection in the exercise of citizenship is not the point of competence. Competence signifies not only the ability to break through barriers to learning but also the ability to deal with the restrictions imposed by the environment and by one's own limitations. In the human world of imperfection, acknowledging one's own weaknesses and learning to live with them, or having the courage to ask for help in overcoming them, perhaps constitute a competence that is far more important than the continual and stubborn pursuit of perfection. A certain tolerance in this respect is important not only in one's interaction with other people but also in dealing with oneself.

To act civilly in awkward situations is a crucial citizen skill. Civility, manners, and good taste are more than mere appearances. They codetermine the substantive quality and outcome of political processes. Nadezhda Mandelstam (1974), Edward Shils, Václav Havel, and many other thinkers who are primarily interested in substance have insisted on the importance of the forms of civility. It is true that there are situations in which manners and politeness remain merely outward appearances—or worse, in which they reinforce meanness and injustice in the interaction between people. However, it does not follow that we would be better off without manners. In communities in which manners and civility are shoved aside, people are even more defenseless against meanness and injustice, once the initial euphoria and goodwill that come with direct democracy and genuine human contact have worn thin.

Unfortunately, civility is not only indispensable but also insufficient. It may be powerless against violence, lies, and the unseemly and selfish behavior that so often characterize real political life. Citizen competence, therefore, also entails the ability to deal with these, to know where to draw the line and where to fight the opposite party with its own weapons. This is not easy. In a democracy, at what point should one forbid political parties that undermine democracy? When and how should one react to marines who try to restore order in a railway station by chasing people they suspect of being drug addicts and dealers, with no explicit orders from the authorities?

In some cases, the evil is clear but difficult to combat. Other cases are problematic because of ambiguity in the definition and perception of evil. Gifts, favors, bribery, corruption, and rewards for services rendered may be part of the necessary "greasing" of daily political interaction. Simply ignoring these is the right strategy for citizens in some situations but not in others. Here, too, citizens must know when and how to bend the rules, and where and how to toe the line.

A crucial aspect of keeping the organization of plurality going is the ability to switch within the repertoire when parties are stuck in one field of interaction or frame of reference. For instance, when formal council meetings show no progress, it may help to arrange an informal and secret gathering. Movement and acknowledgment of the identity and position of parties in one frame of reference may help to get things unstuck and moving again in another field. The double frame provides parties with an eccentric position from which they can consider themselves and their relations. Likewise, humor may constitute a quick change of frame of reference that has liberating consequences. When we laugh, when we see the joke, we have something in common. (Even when we discover that we were all laughing but not all about the same thing, this may make us laugh together.)

A most important aspect of citizen competence in all this is the ability to create a context for mutual action. Without a context, there can be no meaning; and without meaning, there can be no human action. Context is for meaning what oxygen is for human life. We breathe whatever air is available. So it is with context. In order to see meaning, we take as context whatever is available. Changing and choosing a different context so that a different meaning becomes possible is a primary skill of citizens. Differences also need a context in order to be perceived and understood as differences. Some sort of context is always present when human intentionality is at work. Differences are never contextless. Changing or enriching the context is a most important step toward organizing differences in a way that befits citizens.

How do innovations in the repertoire of skills come about? Through detailed attention to situations that are felt to be wrong but that cannot be handled well through the existing repertoire. Real and stubborn attention to situations of injustice and defective citizenship may lead to innovation in the ways of dealing with differences. This is generally a painful and drawn-out search process that requires from citizens boldness and civic courage on the one hand and patience and tolerance on the other. These attributes are not easily combined.

Citizens' competence depends not only on other persons but also on the institutional setting, the established ways, within which they act. A corrupt regime or foreign occupation require different actions from citizens than a constitutional state that is functioning normally. Some forms of competence can only prosper in particular institutional settings. Conversely, functioning in certain institutions can lead to occupational disabilities, blindness, and trained incapacity. Readers can provide their own favorite examples—the one-dimensional manager, the honest but obtuse civil servant, or the "law-abiding" concentration camp commander. Institutions are, in turn, dependent on competent use. Useful and citizenship-promoting institutions such as the council of ministers and the parliament can function only if people use them competently. Weak ministers might harm not only themselves and their departments but also the council of ministers and the parliament.

Institutions provide patterns of and for interactions (March and Olsen 1989; Douglas 1987). In plural societies, there are numerous institutions designed to process plurality: the media, the courts, conversation (talking the matter out), therapy, management, a municipal council, a forum, arbitration, mediation, the free press, parliament, and a party congress. Some of these are directed exclusively toward the arbitration of conflicts, others more generally toward organizing plurality. Some institutions offer strictly ordered rituals, while others function more informally. However, the outcome of the processing of plurality is, in principle, never predetermined, not even in the case of rituals. It depends among other things upon the competent contributions of different persons who are involved in the "collision" between different ways of life. The organization of plurality requires from its participants competent improvisation and translation—far more than mere obedience and the blind application of formulas.

The process of organizing plurality between citizens usually at some point involves a solemn occasion, a ritual of sorts that reestablishes and reconfirms the integrity of the parties involved. Such a ritual of purification and reintegration is a reaction to pollution, to the dangers of disruption of the bonds of civility. In liberal democracies, responsibility fora are a prominent form of such rituals. Such fora are activated when situations occur that are experienced as bad and undeservedly painful to people. In the forum the chain of events that led to this situation is reinterpreted as, and linked to, the actions of persons who can be called to account in the forum. Blind history, a chain of events, is retold as a story of human actions. The happenings in the world are seen as the result of decisions of people who can, as citizens, be called to account for what they have done. In the forum they may give, or may be obliged to give, their version of the story. Having heard this, the forum gives its verdict and assigns responsibility. In doing so, it is reinterpreting the past so as to make possible in the future more outspoken human responsibility for unpalatable events. Shocking outcomes bring matters to a forum, where stories are retold, citizens are made into responsible actors, and norms are reset. It is important to notice that in this normative resetting, the voice of the accused citizen has a central place, albeit not a decisive one. The citizen participates not only in the actual organization of plurality, but also in reflecting about the norms by which it should be governed.

Republics must be endowed with a variety of institutions that help members organize their plurality by offering, and sometimes forcing upon them, a repertoire of ways of dealing with plurality. A plural society is inconceivable without such institutions. However, this high-level and differentiated development of institutions also causes problems.

Firstly, the required knowledge and skills are so advanced that the help of experts such as lawyers and judges is indispensable. This in turn requires that laymen be capable of dealing with the experts and of correctly assessing the value of their contributions. This is no simple matter.

Secondly, access to the institutions that process plurality may be problematic—for instance, because of the cost of expertise, or because of differences in power. While one person may have easy access, another may have little or none. In such cases, if citizenship is to be more than a mere formality, the state (or some other instance) must help its citizens. Yet the arrangements made toward that end lead to financial problems for the state and to certain citizens taking undue advantage of such arrangements.

Thirdly, institutions can become obsolete in the sense that they no longer adequately represent plurality. Consequently, their processing of plurality will leave much to be desired. Representation in today's society is increasingly problematic. Schemes of representation can no longer be trusted blindly. They need to be checked and judged with regard to their applicability. Frequently they need some ad hoc adjustment. Judgment as to which scheme of representation can be used sensibly in *this* particular situation of plurality is becoming increasingly important. Are there experts who can help in this, or must citizens rely on their own judgment in this crucial question?

ACCEPTING PLURALITY, BUT NOT BLINDLY

Although it is necessary to go to the micro level to understand what it takes to organize plurality, we cannot stay there. Micro transactions congeal into macro outcomes. Moreover, macro forces may be so strong as to leave no freedom to speak of at the micro level, the level of individual choice and identity.

A micro vision combined with a positive acceptance of plurality may also conceal differential power effects and inequalities resulting from, or reinforced by, such a micro approach. That is another reason to return to the macro level. The generally positive attitude toward existing plurality needs to be qualified, if it leads to outcomes that are unacceptable when viewed in terms of third parties, longer term consequences, and cumulative impact. Citizenship involves more than organizing differences between two persons only.

The central place of plurality in contemporary society can easily lead to blindness in the face of the effects of power. Plurality can be used to reinforce power, by dividing and ruling, by ranking and by categorizing. Listen, for instance, to the conclusion drawn by Benjamin Sijes at the end of a life of political struggle and painstaking research. He asked about the possibilities for resisting the deportation of Dutch Jews during World War II:

> Even if the Jewish citizens had been able to elect a different [Jewish] Council, they would have exercised no choice in the matter, because only a Council that executed German commands would be accepted by the Germans. That is why it did not matter who was to be at the top of *the*, or of *a* Jewish Council. The Jewish citizens existed only through the Jewish Council, that is to say, as administrative units numbered on lists in order to be deported in due time. "Depersonalization"—albeit in the social sense—resulted from the fact that they were isolated. They were no longer "complete" people because they were rejected and in several ways excluded, out of fear, by non-Jews. These Jews no longer were part of the old reality and did not know what to do. More than ever before, they were the plaything of merciless powers, powers they hardly understood. It made them powerless and incapable of action. They could not reach the illegal helpers, who in turn—aside from the real difficulties—could not reach the Jews. And thus, some 80 percent of the Jews met their death. (Sijes 1974:149)

The implication seems to be that the best moment for resisting was when distinctions between kinds of citizens were introduced. At that time, common action by citizens on the basis of their common citizenship was still possible. Later, when injustice became more evident, the basis and moment for common action had disappeared.

When answering the question of whether the power effects of plurality are unacceptable from the point of view of citizens, a distinction can be made between domains: the public-political, the public-social, and the private domains. The first domain is where political and governmental decisions are made concerning (the adjustment of) the organization of society. Equality of citizens as participants and as sources of influence in this process is a core value. Plurality must time and again be constituted and confirmed by the free choice of individual citizens. That is the reason why elections are held periodically and why representatives of the people, once they have been elected, may vote without having to consult their supporters. When plurality has power effects that endanger this freedom (for example, the democratic empowerment of a Hitler), intervention is called for.

The public-social domain refers to the interaction of people in (semi) public areas such as the streets. Here, personal freedom is central: the freedom to come and go as one pleases, and to have a lifestyle of one's own. Rules of decency and civil law order this interaction. They allow considerable plurality and differences in power. From the point of view of citizenship, a line must be drawn only when these differences actually make admission to and exercise of citizenship in the public-political domain impossible. Think, for example, of street terror or of intimidation at the workplace. Still more restraint is required with regard to public intervention in the private domains of the home, friendships, and social clubs. Yet even there, the power effects of plurality can be such that access to citizenship actually remains an illusion.

The distinctions may be illustrated with regard to cultural minorities. Except for their responsibility to abide by the law, (members of) minorities are free to form and maintain communities, as well as to propagate their own culture. A republic that admits plurality will promote this freedom and may even provide means toward that end. Minorities do not have to comply with "the" national culture. The only requirement is that they abide by the law and that they be sufficiently competent to act in the public-political domain. Political integration is obligatory; sociocultural integration is not. Minorities have a right to be protected against the power of the "normal" national culture and ways of life.

There are two situations in which the interference of the republic extends beyond these limits. The first is one in which slavish relationships actually prevent access to the equal status of citizen. The other situation is one in which minority communities display a coercive character and frustrate the civic freedom of members to leave a community. Such effects of the celebration of plurality must be firmly limited by the republic, however difficult this may be, without thereby destroying plurality more than is strictly necessary.

Plurality is the primary focus of the work of citizens. It is basic material that they transform through antagonistic cooperation into a livable political culture. Plurality is disturbing (or outright dangerous) to citizens, and it is the basis on which citizens act. Like fuel, it enables us to move, but it can also catch fire. Plurality in a democratic republic is neither to be embraced nor to be rejected: It must be accepted as a reality that is to be transformed in such a way by those involved that citizenship for all participants in a community of fate is secured.

In this chapter, we have developed a picture of plurality in contemporary society, of the "way we are now." This picture can be marked by three points of recognition:

1. The Unknown Society;
2. "We are all natives now" (Geertz 1983:151));
3. "If a lion could talk, we would not understand him" (Wittgenstein 1958:223).

The first expression reminds us that plurality and difference occupy a central position; that plurality is not given but to be discovered; and that we can learn from the ways people in The Unknown Society have learned to live with plurality. The second statement points out that there are no privileged and general language and rationality at hand within which plurality could be organized in an authoritative manner and that we must translate from one rationality to another. The third statement indicates that a common language alone is not enough to secure mutual understanding, that it is also a question of ways of life and of self-evident ways of acting. The lion is no lamb, nor is he a human being.

FOUR

□ □ □

Against Consensus

In the great majority of studies, discourses, and policies concerning citizenship, consensus occupies a central place. This is understandable: If people agree, then they have no reason to quarrel. The idea then easily follows that by increasing consensus we shall diminish disturbing and disruptive differences. This assumption about the goodness and political desirability of consensus is widespread.

Nevertheless, nagging questions remain. What if people want to differ, even when they agree about many things? What if they search for, or cultivate and create, differences to fight about? Does the idea of a consensual society not run counter to liberal principles of freedom and to the insight that resilience usually resides in diversity? Isn't a consensual society a dead society, cut off from its sources of vitality? Many defenders of consensus as a condition of peaceful living together would grant these points and withdraw to a more modest position. In order to differ peacefully about some things, they would say, people need to agree about other things as "basics," or terms of peace. A certain amount of consensus is a necessary prerequisite for social and political order.

This study disagrees even with the more modest position. The statement that some consensus surely is necessary is either true by definition—an axiom that cannot be proven false—or a statement that can empirically be falsified and that, in fact, is not always true. Consensus, I have become convinced, is neither a necessary nor a sufficient condition for the organization of plurality by citizens in a republic. Let me explain why.

FIT OR CONSENSUS

If a society does not fly apart but somehow holds together, then it must have parts that fit. When we call this fit "consensus," we seem to make an innocent move. Obviously people agree somehow, somewhere, do they not? However, the move is not innocent at all, either normatively or empirically. The term consensus suggests a way of seeing and doing things that those involved would recognize as their own. Consensus need not always be explicit and conscious; but when an implicit consensus is pointed out to those involved, they should confirm that this is what they participated in. Otherwise the label "consensus" would be a misnomer. Consensus always carries connotations of agreement, consent. The behaviors of slave and master fit together, but there is no (human) consensus. We cannot conceive that human beings would consent to such a relationship. Or rather, we do not accept such a relationship as human, and therefore consider there to be something wrong with the humaneness of those who do (seem to) consent to such relationships. Thus, the idea that when behaviors fit together, this indicates, or must be due to, consensus, is untenable. Fit may or may not go together with consensus.

Even when there is consensus, further specification is in order. Is it consensus in values, in lifestyles, in ways of doing that obtain locally (like driving on the right-hand side of the road)? Does consensus stand for sameness, or for fitting together? The pieces of a puzzle fit together, but the fun of the puzzle is precisely that they are not obviously the same or identical. How deep and permanent is the consensus? Consensus has connotations of permanence and reliability over time, but how deep and permanent need it actually be to count as consensus? Not very. When visitors to Amsterdam quarrel with the Dutch, they usually do so in English. There is a consensus to speak this language, but it is neither permanent nor deep. The consensus does not hold in other situations. We have the idea that consensus needs deep and permanent anchoring—in God, a long history, one's innermost convictions, or whatever. Even when metaphysical foundations have become discredited and unstable, people cling to the idea of deep anchoring, which corresponds to the deeply felt human need for a home, roots, continuity, and a livable future. But why should a need, simply because it is deeply felt, have a deep "solution"? However, leaving metaphysical and other certainties behind does not imply that we should embrace arbitrariness and ignore the human need for continuity. The discovery that Dutch is not a universal language, or that Santa Claus does not exist, does not force us to stop speaking Dutch or celebrating Santa Claus's birthday. On the contrary, insight into the contingent character of these particulars invites us to care for their preservation.

We may mislocate the source of consensus. When we shake hands, their forms obviously fit. Is this a consensus between hands? Obviously not. It is the will, the consensus, to shake hands that makes the forms fit. This shows that external fit is not necessarily the source or locus of consensus but rather its result. This insight may, in turn, lead to the equally mistaken assumption that there is always an inner source of consensus that accounts for the external fit. Such an assumption is difficult to refute—when cornered defenders can always switch to another inner source—but it can surely be undermined by looking at how things go in the world. Then we quickly see that consensus about values (things we hold dear, deep down inside) is neither a necessary nor a sufficient condition for peaceful interaction between people. Spouses who agree about a great many values may kill each other (consensus here is not a sufficient condition for peace). There are cultures and situations in which "incomprehensible" strangers are received as guests and friends (not a necessary condition, therefore). The idea that there *must* be a consensus is a requirement of our (way of) thinking, of our grammar (in Wittgenstein's sense). (In a similar vein, our "feeling someone else's pain" is grammatically impossible: Pain that one feels is, by definition, one's own.) We always find the requirement confirmed, that where we find peaceful living together and communication, this "must" be due to a minimum of consensus. (Compare: When I dance with someone, when movements fit together, this must be due to the common rhythm that we hear in our heads and to the band's playing with such swing and such contagious conviction.) What makes you so sure of this "must"? Is it based on experience?

CONDITION OR DESIRED OUTCOME

In those cases in which people succeed in dealing peacefully with differences, values and principles reveal themselves in their actions. Regardless of whether those values were common before the act(ions), they are apparently common now. A successful interaction constitutes a precedent, offering values and principles for future interactions. This way of formulating things acknowledges that preexisting values are not always necessary for peaceful interaction and that the interaction itself can create values. However, this way of formulating things, in my view, still puts too much emphasis on values. It neglects the fact that values and principles, even when firmly established, have to be applied competently and be weighed against conflicting values and principles. It is precisely in times when plurality pops up everywhere that competent handling of conflicts of loyalties and values becomes an indispensable civic virtue. The exercise of this ability also creates precedents, values, and principles. These, however, have a metacharacter, and their application demands situational judgment. They are neither self-evident nor self-executing.

Of course we want a permanent and firm anchoring for institutions that will enable us to deal with conflicts peacefully. But no metaphysical anchoring or justification can prevent such metainstitutions in plural soci-

eties from becoming objects of primary conflict. For organizing such colli-
sions, there is no longer—if there ever was—a single substantive formula
binding all members together. Not only is plurality a practical problem
nowadays, but it pops up everywhere: in metaphysical foundations, in
systems of rules, in social fragmentation. There is no longer one rationality, one administration, one national society. Unity is no longer considered as given—a given that we did not always clearly see but for which
we could search together. Unity now is not expected to come from outside (meta), nor can it be found in society or in systems-steering. The recurrent political task of citizens is to achieve unity by themselves.

In many theories, consensus is conceived of as a necessary condition
for citizens acting together in peace. These views are mistaken. Consensus is not a condition but a problem that citizens have to work on. Consensus is not a precondition but rather a desired outcome of citizen activities. It is on this point that the neorepublican theory of citizenship differs
from other theories. For neorepublicans, the organization of problematic
plurality is a central task, whereas many other conceptions define this
contemporary problematic out of existence by opting for a substantive
description of citizenship, the unity of which is the exact denial of plurality. Their strategy is to emphasize unity in order to reduce plurality to the
point where it ceases to be a problem. The point of neorepublican citizenship is to increase competence in dealing with existing plurality.

If citizenship is to be more than an idea, it needs to be embraced and
practiced by actual people. The wish to foster commitment to citizenship
and civic virtue is understandable and legitimate. But it cannot be fulfilled by postulating the necessity and unavoidability of unity and by
moralizing about it. This is both bad social science and bad politics: bad
social science, because society does not work that way; bad politics, because it is either ineffective or inimical to the idea of political interaction
between a plurality of equal citizens. The appeal to consensus is either too
vague or simply wrong. It is too vague as long as it remains unclear what
it refers to—sameness, fit, acquiescence, or consent—and whether in
ideas or in actual behavior. It is wrong when it assumes the necessity of a
value consensus. No vital contemporary society works that way. It needs
tension, differences, dynamics. The idea that unity of values is essential
conflates a desired result with the conditions for producing it—conditions that are not permanent and that do not always consist in values. The
conditions are, in fact, variable, and they often have no connection with
values, whether deeply held and shared or not.

When it is said that Holland is a "consensus society," this calls up a picture of agreement as a normal and permanent condition of society, of consensus as something given, a starting point. This picture is mistaken. It
obscures that Dutch people are used to working hard to produce consen-

sus, to transforming and defining their differences in such a way that all can agree to live with them. Such agreement can be called "consensus." When it is often aimed for and achieved, we may speak of a "consensus society"—however, without forgetting that this indicates a desirable outcome of citizen interaction and not a precondition for it.

CULTURAL FACTS

Why is it that the consensus assumption is so widespread? This may have to do with the way people conceive of "'cultural facts." Cultural facts are facts that would not exist without human agreement—marriage, soccer, puberty, an order, law, money. They are ontologically subjective (Searle 1996), because their existence depends on what human subjects do and intend. In this they differ from ontologically objective facts, like a thunderstorm or the moon, which are what they are regardless of what human beings think and do. Ontological subjectivity and objectivity must be distinguished from epistemic subjectivity and objectivity (Searle 1996:8). Taste is epistemically subjective; an observation that can be corrected is epistemically objective. Correct use of an established language, such as English, is epistemically objective and ontologically subjective. Cultural facts get their solid, objective "hardness" (we cannot change them at will) through the "soft" (culturally and historically variable) activities and interpretations made by human subjects. When these activities and interpretations stop or change, the cultural facts cease to be (what they were). When words, for instance, cease to be taken or "counted" as an order by those involved, they cease being an order.

This character of cultural facts, once it is appreciated, makes it tempting to see them as based on consensus in the sense of shared normative convictions of all subjects who are involved in the "creation" of those facts. However, their involvement need not be normative at all. Most people are realistic; they are not going to deny the existence of facts. They stick to the facts, regardless of whether these are "natural" (ontologically objective) or cultural (ontologically subjective). I speak Dutch because that is the language normally used in the country where I live; I use Dutch postage stamps because that is what it takes to send a letter—not because I hold a certain value or norm but because that is what the cultural facts are where I live. Through my behavior, I contribute to the continued existence of those cultural facts; but it is mistaken to see in this a consensus on norms and values. Such normative consensus may or may not be there, empirically, among some of the people involved. But who acts out of inner conviction and who out of realistic conformism is difficult to sort out as long as the cultural facts are firmly established.

This reality changes when cultural facts, for whatever reason or through whatever incident, begin to lose their self-evident character. Then earlier motivations are revealed. Those people who before, out of realism, supported those facts through their actual behavior, will stop doing so. To say that they have lost or changed values and norms is mistaken, because these never played a role to begin with. Those who valued the cultural facts in question will try to stick to the behavior that supported them—as will, for a while, those who act from routine and tradition.

Many people, it seems to me, stick to cultural facts not because they agree with them normatively but because these facts are so well established that disagreeing makes no sense. It is not consensus, an inner conviction, but realism that motivates them. It is their realism that results in a conformity in behavior, that we are tempted to interpret as originating in an inner conviction or a consensus.

FIVE

□ □ □

Deep Groups Under
a Multicultural Surface

We have argued that plurality is not given but socially constructed and that conflicts in loyalties are normal occurrences in the lives of citizens. However, in some societies and in certain periods we do not find variable plurality and conflicts but permanent groups separated by unbridgeable cleavages. Plurality seems to have frozen into hard groups, whose chilly relations are reinforced through repetitive social construction. Temporary conflicts seem to have become permanent enmities. The organization of plurality is failing, again and again. This chapter considers such situations. Many observers have assumed that they constitute the "normal" state societies are in. Earlier, we argued that regardless of whether this was so in the past, at present, plurality is much more fleeting and variable. The historical movement is toward a pluralization of plurality. (Lately, as in Bosnia, this movement seems to have changed direction, groups having become locked again into permanent enmity. Further on in this chapter, I show how this change may be understood to arise out of the broader movement of pluralization.) Nevertheless, fixation into permanent group opposition does occur also in present-day societies and poses a serious challenge to the viability of citizenship as a principle of public order.

DEEP GROUPS

Three characteristics make such situations intractable for neorepublicans. Firstly, being a member of a group (and not primarily an individual) dominates social perception and social relations. Assignment to membership takes place, quasi-automatically or compulsively, on the basis of visible characteristics (skin, gender) and recognizable ways of living. Usually group membership also dominates self-perception. But even when it does not, the social classification is so self-evident and dominant that one can hardly escape it: "You can never forget that you are black." "They never let you forget that you are a woman." Secondly, instead of the normal conflicts between the demands of citizenship and those of other roles and offices—the normal conflicts of loyalty in a differentiated and plural society—we find a permanent rejection of, or incompatibility with, part of the requirements of citizenship. The group members are not, or do not behave as, full citizens. Thirdly, their being less than full citizens is not purely a result of exclusion against their will. Their group membership is "willed" in some sense—if not chosen, then at least accepted as an ineluctable part of what constitutes their identity, of who they are. The group membership functions as the context of meaning, the self-evident setting, within which choice is at all possible. Without that context, there would not even be a choosing self, so to say. Group membership has become a primary reality—take that away, and you deprive people of the world they live in and make sense of.

How does the neorepublican perspective deal with this reality of "deep" group membership that conflicts with the requirements of citizens living together in the republic? First, by giving up the claims of exclusiveness that characterized earlier conceptions of communitarian or republican citizenship. In the neorepublican view, claims of citizenship need not always have priority over the obligations of other offices and roles. Also, neorepublicans accept that multiple citizenship—for instance, simultaneous citizenship of The Netherlands, of Turkey, and of the European Union—has become commonplace. Conflicts between the demands of different republics of which one and the same person is a member are considered less and less often in exclusive ideological terms of sovereignty or what have you. They are pragmatically regulated through treaties, diplomatic compromises, and court decisions—that is, if anyone actually bothers to sort out the details.

However, regardless of whether there is official multiple citizenship or not, the position of (members of) groups inside the republic whose actions and convictions conflict with the minimum requirements of citizenship cannot so easily be accommodated by redefinition and by deideologizing conceptions of citizenship. Groups that are visibly characterized by the way they are oppressed, the way they intimidate, the way they live, the way they look or smell—"guest" workers, mafiosi, women, Indians, Mormons, Muslims, or white male executives—won't go away or change their relations with other citizens through redefinition. They pose problems that extend beyond the conceptual level.

But why exactly do they pose problems at all for the republic? Why not live and let live in the multicultural peace of plurality? Because such fixed and separate group life may conflict with citizenship in various ways— not at its pragmatic periphery, but at its core. The republic wants choice for its citizens. Choice of one's own way of life. For choice to exist, however, alternative ways of life—cultures—need to be reproduced. Should the republic provide extra protection to vulnerable cultures? I cannot choose to speak a language that nobody speaks. In order to know what a way of life entails, lengthy education may be needed. The only way to know what it is to be a guru or a musician is to devote one's life to it, entirely or for a considerable number of years. Citizens should be free to move in and out of ways of life; but how can this freedom be ensured, when the way of life itself constitutes the context of meaning within which choice takes place, and when years of discipline might be required to begin to appreciate what the way of life entails? Sometimes, choice is difficult to realize. Transsexual operations, changing the color of one's skin, or acquiring a new language as a native tongue are at best (or at worst?) only possible for the few (such as Michael Jackson). Being a member of a group, however much appreciated—as with women—may give disadvantages that citizens ought not to have. Group life itself may involve relations in which some are permanently powerless and intimidated. Their position verges on slavery, which may be defined as a situation of long-term powerlessness. However freely chosen, slavery is not an option on the menu of democratic citizenship.

COMMUNITY OF FATE

These considerations illustrate the incompatibility of citizenship with certain forms of separate group life. The neorepublican perspective allows for more and a wider variety of ways of life than most earlier conceptions of citizenship; but its acceptance of plurality does not extend to those forms of behavior that make the organization of differences among citizens itself impossible. But again: Why not leave the groups that do not fit alone? Why should not all go their own way? Why not let them have their own way of life, in their own "republic"? Because the lives of group members and those of the other citizens are connected—by history, chance, earlier choice, or future prospects—in a community of fate. They cannot avoid each other without depriving themselves of what is essential for their way of life (for instance, water supply, a viable economy, institutions of learning, military protection, a judicial system, and territory). They share a community of fate but disagree about the terms on which it can be transformed into a republic that is willed by its own members, its citizens. There is disagreement about the meaning of membership that runs as deep as the level of what we call "identity," of who we are.

A community of fate obtains when people are connected in ways they cannot avoid—bodily (or in symbolic space that works as directly as bodily presence) and also systemically (for instance, through environmental connections). The community of fate is a "given" in the sense that we cannot avoid it. But it only appears and is only experienced by way of a particular cultural interpretation. People on the territory are a given. Whether they are treated as fellow citizens or deported and killed in gas chambers is culturally variable. The primary given is people bumping into each other. It is this given, this chance event that could have been otherwise, to which citizenship is an answer—an answer that transforms the given into the chosen, or at least the accepted. Citizenship generates areas of choice, although it is not usually chosen but rather given. What choice is there in having to die for the country you happen to have been born in (or where your grandparents or your former masters/slaveholders were born, as in the case of American soldiers in Europe during World War II)? Citizens in the republic consider chance worthy of determining their fate, to paraphrase Freud (Rorty 1989:22). The recurrent task of citizens is to transform the "given" encounters between people into relations that are accepted by citizens. In order to achieve this, citizens must again and again reproduce citizenship and the conditions in which it can arise.

Logically, however, this transformation must be preceded by the perception of a "given" community of fate. Such communities are not given in the way stones and plane crashes are. People may fail to notice other people. (When such individuals are accused of having violated human rights—or of having done nothing to stop the violation—their blindness enables them to say in retrospect that they did not know the violation was taking place.) The perception of people "bumping into" each other is dependent on the culture of the perceiver, that is true; but once it has been perceived, it *is* a given that cannot be wished or defined away. How and where, then, do republics perceive the community of people that is to be transformed into citizens? In their practices of admission and exclusion— by deciding who is to be admitted or excluded as a citizen—republics not only define what it is to be a citizen but also circumscribe the community of fate—that is, the set of people who because of their place on earth and in history, qualify as aspiring citizens. The community of fate that forms the given substance of citizenship is further defined by the way in which aspiring citizens are included. They may be put in special camps, interrogated by the police, required to take language courses, welcomed as valuable experts or as cleaners of offices after working hours. In short, they acquire a place in social and administrative hierarchies. But if they are to be citizens, there must be inside that hierarchy one sphere were they are equals and to which access is never closed off for a long period: the public, political sphere, where equality between citizens is again and again to be reconstituted. Citizenship is a position, an office within a hierarchy, which gives individuals an equal voice that is heeded and effective even in the presence of structures of inequality.

EXCLUSIVE CULTURES

Earlier, I explained why the republic cannot allow each and every group its own definition of citizenship (because the continuation of their separate forms of life depends on the organization of the community of fate that they share). However, these factors do not explain why communities of fate are perceived today in such divisive and antagonistic ways by their members. Groups of people increasingly celebrate and insist on their own identities and cultures. States, in turn, are tightening the rules of access to citizenship and insisting on the uniqueness of the (culture of the) nation. Religious affiliation is on the rise as a factor defining one's position in the public sphere. Why are we witnessing this tightening of the cultural bonds of the local and the special in a world that was supposed to be "globalizing," becoming less rigidly hierarchical and more tolerant of differences? Surprisingly, in France and quite a few other countries, the question of admission to citizenship is most vehemently posed where it matters least: with regard to those who are already on the territory and who are in the labor market and the social security system (Brubaker 1992:181). Unlike potential immigrants, actual immigrants do not need citizen status to gain access to coveted positions in welfare states. Granting them citizenship does not "cost" the established citizenry any money. Why, then, do citizens resist the granting of citizenship to immigrants?

The new emphasis on culture and identity may be understood as arising out of the pluralization of social relations, rather than as contradicting it. My argument is as follows: When hierarchical rules and constrictions become weak and when plurality and individualism become more prevalent, groups are no longer primarily reproduced by having a place in a given hierarchy. In order to survive, they must constantly redefine and reconfirm themselves. It is conviction, culture, and right thinking that hold them together. Groups—or states—that feel that their place in the world is not secure and not automatically reproduced resort to such strategies of cultural reproduction. If nothing else holds "us" together, then a common core, an identity, should do the job. Heated talk and violent fights about identity, about who "we" are, arise precisely where such identity is not an easy and self-evident reality. When such conflicts arise, sects quarrel and split; bigger churches establish hierarchies. Sects quarrel about right thinking and are divided by their very effort to maintain the community of equally true believers (where none is holier than another): Their members believe that only right thinking can hold the group together. Hierarchies, in contrast, are held together by established rules and institutions that provide separate compartments for all kinds of thinking and dissidence. They do not split; they differentiate.

This understanding of the increasing emphasis on culture and identity in our times is, of course, not compelling, because it does not meet the Popperian criterion of falsifiability. It understands both pluralization and its apparent opposite, the new cultural exclusiveness, in terms of the same continuing trend of dehierarchization. However, it has the merit of at least making some sense out of the strong emphasis on culture and identity that characterizes our time.

PRINCIPLES FOR MULTICULTURAL PRACTICE

What repertoire does the neorepublican perspective offer for coping with cultural diversity and exclusiveness? Firstly, it squarely refuses to let itself be drawn into the maelstrom of cultural exclusiveness. It rejects the demand that a supposedly unique national culture be the basis of living together. Secondly, it accepts plurality as a basic given in contemporary societies that should be organized and not mitigated or wished away by the actions and demands of citizens. This point of departure makes it easier for neorepublicans to accept multiple citizenship than it was for adherents of pre-1989 conceptions of citizenship. Thirdly, neorepublicans' focus on practical competence in the organization of plurality rather than on right principles alone gives them an eagerness to learn from practice and a pleasure in innovation (inventing new combinations of practices). Such pragmatic flexibility is often missing in older notions of citizenship according to which theory and practice might diverge, but such divergence had no place in the theory itself. The neorepublican perspective, in contrast, has a theoretical place for the practical activities and developing competences of citizens in action.

Practical arrangements that have developed for dealing with semipermanent incompatibilities between citizenship and other cultural loyalties are studied not only as to their principles but also as to what is required to bring them about, as to *how* people coproduced them. Think, for instance, about arrangements for conscientious objections to military service, or for refusals of inoculation; of consociational arrangements in The Netherlands; and of relations between churches and states. What is interesting here is not primarily the principles but rather the competences of all involved in the making of compromises, while they disagreed on crucial principles. In Russia, politicians might want to create coalitions, but often fail—in part, because they simply lack the practical know-how. Of course, the neorepublican perspective does not reject principles altogether. In this book I have formulated principles that may be used both as guides for practical orientation and as constraints on what kinds of plurality should be tolerated. However, the bottleneck for effective citizenship lies not so much with principles as with using them skillfully in a diversity of practical situations, of people and groups "bumping" into each other.

Some have argued for special public rights for "identity" groups as such, distinct from the rights of individual citizens: cultural rights, rights to group representation in politics and to self-government. Kymlicka (1995:27–33), for instance, distinguishes among three forms of group-differentiated rights—polyethnic rights, special representation rights, and self-government rights. Here, also, the neorepublican perspective emphasizes practical competence and compromise. It rejects such rights in principle, in the sense that if free to choose, it would rather grant rights only to citizens as such. However, there is never, except in theory, such a freedom to choose. Citizens, whether ruling or being ruled, always find themselves in a situation of given plurality and differences that they have not chosen but that they have to work on with citizenship for all as a guideline. The neorepublican view does not make first principles all-important; instead, it emphasizes the principle of practical competence in organizing plurality. It will quite readily accept special cultural rights, if these do not create too many new inequalities and conflicts. Special practices, such as the religiously correct killing of animals, will be allowed, but only in buildings and in settings where offense and visibility to others is minimal. In The Netherlands, private schools organized around particular educational and religious views are publicly financed on an equal footing with public education.

Special group rights in political representation are less easily accepted from the neorepublican point of view. The citizens themselves should form groups and be free to exit from them. If group life in the public-social and the public-political realms is not sustained by the activities of a sufficient number of free citizens, there must be good and compelling grounds for maintaining groups along other routes. Such grounds may be found in the preservation of cultures and ways of life for future generations, in structural disadvantages for members that extend into the public-political realm itself, and in the unavailability of alternative ways to maintain civil peace (as in South Africa).

Rights of self-government, finally, are very unattractive from a neorepublican perspective. They are only appropriate where the community of fate has already split up, or where splitting it up is not too difficult, costly, and unjust. Granting self-government where the community of fate remains intact and tight is a recipe for inefficiency and conflicts like those we have witnessed in Yugoslavia. Such a policy takes away the status of the participants as equal citizens precisely where the protection of minority voices is most needed.

The preferred state of affairs from the neorepublican point of view is that members of "deep" groups participate *as citizens*. This includes their right to bring about, through political and legal argument and decision, changes in the position of their groups. It also includes their right to bring about, through political and legal argument and decision, changes in the rules of the political and legal spheres themselves—and ultimately, in the prevailing and operative conception of citizenship.

SIX

□   □   □

Citizens in Public Office

In 1992, Czechoslovak President Václav Havel (1992:6–8) wrote of the requirements for effective political leadership:

> What you need is tact, the proper instincts, and good taste. One surprising experience from "high politics" is this: I have discovered that good taste is more important than a postgraduate degree in political science. It is essentially a matter of form: knowing how long to speak, when to begin and when to finish, how to say something politely that your opposite number might not want to hear, how to say, always, what is most essential in a given moment, and not to speak of what is not essential or uninteresting, how to insist on your own position without offending, how to create the kind of friendly atmosphere that makes complex negotiations easier, how to keep a conversation going without prying or, on the contrary, without being aloof, how to balance serious political themes with lighter, more relaxing topics, how to plan one's journeys judiciously and how to know when it is more appropriate not to go somewhere, when to be open and when reticent, and to what degree.

How does this emphasis on civility relate to the violence, lies, and unseemly and selfish behavior said to be so common in politics? Havel provided a simple answer: "But it is simply not true that a politician must lie or intrigue. That is utter nonsense, very often spread about by people who—for whatever reason—wish to discourage others from taking an interest in public affairs. . . . It is not true that only the unfeeling cynic, the vain, the brash, and the vulgar can succeed in politics; all such people, it is true, are drawn to politics, but in the end, decorum and good taste will always count for more."

He had to reconsider his answer, however:

> This is what I wrote (some months ago) when I tried to review the experience I had gained during my presidency. At the time I had no way of knowing that I would soon find that there were occasions when it was indeed difficult to go

67

that route. . . . But I still believe that politics, in its very essence, does not necessarily require one to behave immorally. My latest experience, however, confirms the truth of something that, until some weeks ago, I did not really appreciate—that the way of truly moral politics is not simple, or easy.

RULING COCITIZENS

Havel's experience is exemplary for the problems experienced by citizens who want to serve their republic by holding public office. This chapter focuses on the special opportunities and problems of combining general citizenship with a particular public office. If citizenship entails being ruled by cocitizens, then the way they exercise public authority is of central importance: Citizen competence must reveal itself there, if anywhere. However, the combination of citizenship and public office is not only central but also problematic. When exercising special public authority, citizens are allowed or required to do things that as ordinary citizens they are forbidden to do. Policemen use violence and deprive cocitizens of their freedom; judges decide on matters of life and death; members of parliament change the laws that as ordinary citizens, they have to obey; and a general exposes his men to extraordinary risks. Given the different obligations of citizens and public officers, it is understandable that their close combination is seldom emphasized.

The connection is usually considered in terms of democracy and law. The citizen votes; chosen representatives decide; and their democratic decisions are implemented by officeholders who can, if necessary, be corrected by citizens (and other legal subjects, such as firms) through courts of law. In my view, this model is laudable but offers too little. It leaves the citizenship of those who hold public office and exercise the power of the sword over their fellow citizens out of view. Citizenship should make a difference in the exercise of authority in all regions of the public domain. And it should do so not only by providing "ordinary" citizens with rights of refusal and resistance but also by allowing occupants of public office to exercise their citizenship while doing their work. Citizenship should appear and work not only *against* but also *in* public office. It involves both knowing how to rule and how to be ruled. If citizenship stops where particular public authority begins, then it cannot have much effect.

This emphasis on the citizenship of officeholders is not common. Usually the focus is on the "ordinary" citizen, whose ordinariness precisely consists in his not holding any particular office. The mere, naked citizen is posited opposite the holders of office. There were good grounds for such a conceptualization in historical situations in which citizenship for all was not yet an established constitutional principle, as for example, in France under the old regime or in Czechoslovakia between 1968 and 1989. Once the principle is accepted, however, such a conceptualization is counterproductive and misses a most important point of citizenship. It is counterproductive because efforts to improve the position of "ordinary" citizens can never move beyond generalities. The ordinary citizen is the one who is, by definition, without special powers. Insofar as the effort to provide him or her with special powers succeeds, he or she ceases, by definition, to be an ordinary citizen. The conceptualization of the citizen as "ordinary" misses an important point by neatly separating the roles of citizen and officeholder. Such a separation may be convenient, but it defines away the very problems of conflicting loyalties and the organization of plurality, on which citizenship is supposed to work.

For neorepublicans, citizenship is not a safe and separate possession but rather is hammered out and given shape in dealing with disturbing and surprising differences. The plurality that citizens organize obtains not only between individuals and other entities in public-social space but also between offices in public-political space. The demands of these offices may conflict; and in deciding how to deal with such conflict, citizenship should be a guiding principle. In order to highlight this, I have conceptualized citizenship as an *office* among other offices.

Citizenship is not only defined and given shape by special institutions and rules for citizenship, but also in the exercise of other offices, and in institutions that are primarily centered around concerns other than those of citizenship. It is in the organization of the plurality of offices that we (continue to) show, learn, and discover what citizenship is. Citizenship is developed not only when the demands of (the office of) citizenship conflict with those of other public offices but also when various special public officers—for instance, a cabinet minister and a general or the head of the secret service—disagree about what their responsibilities are. Citizenship in this view is a criterion for orientation and evaluation in the exercise of public office and the design of public institutions.

In 1992, the Dutch Scientific Council on Government Policy commissioned studies to flesh out and test this view (Van Gunsteren and Den Hoed 1992). Scholars with expertise in a diversity of practices were asked to report what orientation—if any—the neorepublican conception of citizenship provided in the particular practice they were concerned with. Most questions and reports concerned practices and roles in the public-political sphere (tax inspector, soldier, policeman, civil servant under foreign occupation, public relations officer, head of the internal security service). Some reports concerned practices and roles in the public-social sphere (journalist, teacher, unemployed worker). In the following discussion, I have drawn upon these earlier studies. I have left aside the studies of other societal practices and roles—for instance, drug addicts, mentally handicapped persons, or children—in which those involved are insufficiently capable of ruling and therefore are "incomplete" citizens. Their position poses different problems.

What is at stake in the relations between citizens and public office? Historically, the demand for protection against arbitrary rule usually came first, closely followed by the demand for equality before the law—that is, for one regime of known laws that applies to all persons equally. Later came the demand for democracy, for a say in making and changing the content of the laws, which was closely followed by the demand for democratic control over policymaking and over administrative implementation of the laws. It has become clear to many that this kind of remote control is at present insufficient to ensure the rule of citizens over citizens. In turbulent situations, administrators simply have too much leeway, too much discretionary power. To keep administration on the republican track, therefore, we want it to be in the hands of cocitizens who do not completely bracket their citizenship but rather, remember while ruling, what it is to be ruled; cocitizens who can stay the course of citizenship even while navigating in turbulent waters. A growing number of scholars of democratic governance insist that retrospectively holding rulers responsible is no longer sufficient to guide most of their public activities. Ordinary citizens expect rulers to use citizenship as a compass in unknown waters, but without neglecting the special rules and requirements of their particular offices. In quieter times, it could still be assumed that those rules and requirements were such that sticking to them would also be the best way to realize citizenship. Nowadays, when administrators are more frequently confronted with the unexpected and the unknown, conflicts between the demands of citizenship and those of special offices are sharper and more frequent. How are citizens who occupy special offices to deal with these?

EXTREME SITUATIONS

It may be helpful to begin with an extreme case—that of civil servants in the Netherlands under German occupation, during World War II—where the contours of the problem are retrospectively magnified. After the war, a number of civil servants were brought to trial before courts and investigative committees for alleged wrongdoings they had committed as civil servants during the foreign occupation. But what exactly had they done wrong, and under what rules and in what capacity were they being tried (Den Hoed 1992)? In many cases, they had broken no criminal law, committed no crime against humanity, and violated no explicit rule governing their office. Nevertheless, their behavior during the war was deemed to be wrong and they were disciplined, demoted, or fired. On what grounds? The proceedings and punishments begin to make sense when we see them in terms of citizenship. Civil servants were held accountable as citizens who failed to do what is required of citizens in the particular situation they were in—that of civil servants under foreign occupation and rule. Fate had brought them into a difficult situation, in which they failed to do what was necessary to maintain the community of fate that obtained between citizens. Many civil servants who were found guilty were convicted not because of their membership in a particular organization of collaborators, nor because they served a foreign power, but because they failed to act adequately as the "shield and sword" of the citizens. The judges argued that they should have protected citizens more effectively against the German authorities. Another wrongdoing, according to the courts, consisted in their having led citizens astray by setting a bad example: By collaborating with the occupiers, the civil servants had created the impression that this behavior was right, that this was the thing to do. They had failed to act as exemplary citizens.

Another extreme case is that of the secret service that is supposed to monitor and protect the republic against internal subversion. At issue here is not foreign occupation but the "no go" areas that ought to be, or that seem to be, ruled by the law and its sword but in fact are not. The director of the Dutch security service in 1992 wrote an article tellingly titled "Citizenship in extremis" (Docters van Leeuwen 1992). Security services use the worst of means, such as asking citizens to inform against each other, or disseminating knowledge about someone without opportunity for rebuttal, toward a laudable end—the security of the democratic state and the rule of law. The latter, in turn, form the framework within which citizenship can be exercised. But instead of protecting citizens, security services often have done the reverse. They have a bad reputation because they have, as with Napoleon and Fouché or the Stasi in East Germany, been used to protect the state *against* legitimate activities of its citizens.

The existence in and of a security service is full of paradoxes and dilemmas. In order to protect a democratic process, a security service is created the actions of which are surrounded by a secrecy that, in turn, runs counter to democratic openness and public debate. When, on what grounds, is a security operation that may impinge heavily on the lives of citizens to be started? Mere rumors are not enough. But what if they concern matters that, if true, are very serious? When is it time to stop an operation? These are all questions of proportionality that demand judgment and "virtual" citizenship, that is thinking in terms of citizenship and public debate in situations where these cannot fully unfold. In a democratic-constitutional state, cooperation of citizens with the security service is voluntary. May the service accept such cooperation when this puts the citizen in acute danger of which he or she is insufficiently aware? To whom and how should the service report? If only those who "need to know" are informed, there is ample room for manipulation. At least a few persons outside the service should have an overview and be fully informed. This still leaves us with a situation in which a few know "everything"; a small number, much; a larger number, something; and many, nothing. This is highly undesirable. The security service should, therefore, not be exempted from public debate. It is difficult to sail between the Scylla of openness and the Charybdis of secrecy; yet it is precisely in such situations—where the democratic process is defective and the leeway for judgment and deception great—that citizenship is needed, that we want to feel that we are ruled by cocitizens.

HOW NORMAL?

The cases of citizens in public office that we have considered thus far concern situations of extremity in which the normal functioning of the republic, including its rules of office, is defective or has been suspended. In such situations, citizenship functions as a kind of alternative site or building block from which the republic can be reconstituted. But what bearing does this have on normal situations? Quite a lot. First of all, it sharpens our awareness of dangers lurking in apparently normal situations. (This may also make people oversuspicious and thereby undermine the republic. However, perception and awareness need not automatically lead to action. Judgment and wisdom lie in knowing when *not* to react. This is precisely what reflection on the security service may show.) Secondly, by seeing distinctions magnified in extreme situations, citizens may learn to make finer distinctions and to judge in quieter, everyday situations as well. Thirdly, the normal is no longer as normal as it used to be. We live, it is said, in turbulent times—times in which tradition, self-evident context, and "business as usual" more and more often prove unreliable or insufficient guides for action. For many people the unstructured, the extraordinary, the surprising, and the unknown have become normal occurrences, to be expected as part of daily life. This does not mean that we should discard traditional procedures or take the rules that govern the functioning of public office lightly, acting as if we were always in extreme situations: People cannot, or at least should not, be asked or forced to live that way. It is, however, an argument to more creatively and frequently use citizenship to keep things on their "normal" course in the republic—"normal" here meaning both normative and usual.

The relation between citizenship and other public offices in the republic is in fact an old theme. The right to bear arms and serve in a citizen army;

the right to a fair trial, to an adversary procedure in which the accused has equal standing with the accusers and judges; and the principle of no taxation without representation were central in the establishment of earlier republics. Citizens acquired some standing against public authority that earlier was exercised *over* them as subjects without their consent. What is primarily at stake nowadays in a neorepublican perspective is, however, citizenship *in* the exercise of public authority, citizenship as a constitutive principle for design of and judgment in public office.

Jacques van Doorn (1992) has argued, in his study "Citizens in Uniform," that the citizen who decides to be a soldier and therefore is willing to bear the furthest reaching consequence of his citizenship (i.e., death) chooses a special status. Citizenship assumes, after all, a certain degree of freedom and independence, whereas for soldiers, loyalty to one's own organization takes priority. Van Doorn questioned whether compulsory military service should be regarded as a duty of citizenship. The system of general, compulsory military service ensures that the responsibility for maintaining the political community is evenly distributed. Military service is regarded as a manifestation of dedicated participation in a crucial activity of that same community and is part of the education young people receive to become responsible citizens. In that view, compulsory military service is a civic duty. And yet many democracies have trouble with it or even reject it. Apparently, military service is regarded as an instrument of the state rather than as a manifestation of citizenship. Many people do not acknowledge a citizen duty to serve in an organization in which so many citizen rights are bracketed. Current social developments confirm this. The bond between citizen and army is loosening, and the defense of the country is left to a specialized force.

Formally, the soldier is a citizen. In reality, however, the practice of citizenship within the army appears extremely problematic. The army aims to impose its will on the enemy by way of (the threat) of massive violence. Its structure is geared toward this goal: It is hierarchical, disciplined, formal, target-oriented, and isolated. As experience has shown, such centrally led organizations tend to discourage and limit the expression of citizenship by their members; and indeed, the army leaves its members little room for the exercise of citizenship, either inside or outside the organization. The tension that is observed between military service and citizenship will have to be accepted, however, because the army can pose as great a danger to the republic when it has too much citizenship as when it has too little: If the army is to be an effective fighting force, its members cannot be permitted individually to assess the legality or legitimacy of a given assignment and to act according to their separate assessments. Thus, whether a low degree of citizenship in the army actually puts the republic at risk necessarily depends more on the maturity of the political order within which and on behalf of which the army functions than on the army itself. Nevertheless, we expect our cocitizens who serve in the armed forces to remember their citizenship at the same time as they obey military rules and political authorities, and to give the demands of citizenship priority on occasions when they conflict with the demands of the latter, as in the cases of crimes against humanity or of antidemocratic political instructions.

Likewise, we expect policemen and prosecutors to follow the legal rules governing their offices but also not to forget what it is to be a citizen who is being ruled. In other words, they must take the rules seriously but not as absolute and exclusive guides. This is no easy assignment. The obligation of policemen and prosecutors to treat alleged trespassers of the law as cocitizens and not as people (who have placed themselves) outside the protection of the legal order is also not easy to fulfill. Talk about "criminals" as if they were another kind of being comes easily, but it is wrong. The legal order knows no "criminals" but only citizens or legal subjects who have violated a law. The violator is within the legal order and therefore is punished as a responsible citizen. People who because of some defect—because they are in some way different beings—cannot be held responsible are not punished but are put away in special institutions such as asylums, where they are treated and kept. The primary point of police work and prosecution is not exclusion but maintenance of the legal order. This is too easily forgotten by officeholders at all levels who are no longer guided by memory or imagination of what it is to be on the other side of office, among those who are being ruled by it ('t Hart 1994). They have forgotten their common citizenship.

Like soldiers and policemen, tax inspectors today are professionals whose income no longer depends on the amount of taxes that they extort from the king's subjects. They are officials who according to rules made by the citizens' representatives in parliament, determine what their cocitizens must pay. However, in a turbulent world, those rules leave ample and increasing room for interpretation and discretion. How are inspectors to act? In recent decades, in The Netherlands, the answer has been given in terms of an efficiently managed and "productive" organization. The Internal Revenue Service has taken the corporation as its guiding model for reorganizing itself. Ed van der Ouderaa (1992) points out that tax inspectors thereby lose their independent position and with it the possibility of exercising citizenship in their office. In the redesign of the internal revenue service, the citizens were conceived of as clients and the citizenship of the inspector in the fulfillment of his office was forgotten. If citizenship is to play a role in the fulfillment of office, it should also be a principle in the design and (re)organization of that office.

Until recently, the political arena was largely dominated by the power of the word, the sword, and money. In the twentieth century, two other kinds of power have risen to the fore: organization and knowledge. The power of organization was recognized by revolutionaries such as Lenin, by businessmen, and by politicians who organized their parties. The question of what responsibilities citizens who are managers of organizations have, became painfully loud when Nazi leader Karl Adolf Eichmann, an organizer of the extermination of Jews, defended himself against accusations of war crimes by pointing out that he personally had never wished the Jews ill; that he himself had not murdered Jews; and that he had done nothing but follow legal rules and regulations. The power of knowledge is on the rise and is expected to increase in the age of information that we are now entering. Robert Reich (1991) considers symbolic analysts, those who can understand and rearrange symbols, the primary generators of economic growth and income (for themselves and for others). The responsibility of citizens who have access to technical knowledge is a hotly contested issue. Cases in point are that of the German rocket scientists, among them Werner von Braun, who were brought to the United States after World War II and granted U.S. citizenship in return for developing a new generation of weapons; and that of Robert Oppenheimer, who headed the team that built the first atomic bomb and who was subsequently accused of un-American conduct. Another shining example is the Russian scientist and dissident Andrei Sakharov. Questions concerning these leading scientists' responsibilities as citizens, which are often rather unilluminatingly debated in moral terms, can, I submit, become somewhat more tractable when citizenship is defined as a public office. The similar responsibilities of other symbolic analysts—of the communicators who carry important messages to the public and of the new rhetoricians who manipulate these media—are equally great. U.S. President Ronald Reagan often has been praised as "the great communicator"; but Mikhail Gorbachev's similar success in communication was compared by German Chancellor Helmut Kohl to that of Paul Joseph Goebbels, the Nazi minister of propaganda. Goebbels the communicator, Von Braun the scientist, Eichmann the organizer: This trio shows how reflecting on the documented experience of Hitler's Germany can help clarify the responsibilities of citizens in high public office today.

The question of citizenship can be posed not only with regard to occupants of office in public-political space but also with a view to the roles and functions that people fulfill in society, in what we earlier called public-social space. Think of a journalist, a lawyer, members of the board of a foundation, a soccer referee, an engineer who is in charge of daily operations and security at a nuclear plant, or the president of a conglomerate of which one firm violates a weapons boycott or elementary safety precautions. Each may, suddenly and without having chosen to do so, find himself in a situation in which cocitizens demand, or will retrospectively demand, that he remember his citizenship and bring it to bear on the way he fulfills his special function. Obviously, such demands often are unwelcome. One would rather ignore them, or not have heard them, if only because it is so difficult to invent a suitable response. To practice citizenship in such offices is more difficult than it is in the voting booth. However, actors in public-social space do find orientation in civil law and court decisions, which tell them, through a rich kaleidoscope of cases, what they may reasonably expect from each other and themselves. Civil law tells them what treating the others as equal participants in civil interaction entails—in what ways they are obliged to take into account other persons and their goods.

DISTURBING DEMANDS

This chapter does not provide an exhaustive overview of citizenship in public offices and roles. That would require more study and attention to differences of meaning by country and era. The above serves merely to develop some idea of what is involved. It is a first exercise from an angle that is usually ignored. The exploration yields some conclusions.

Without normality, without things that can be taken for granted, good interaction and safe existence are not possible. This valuable insight, however, does not show us which, or more precisely, whose things that are taken for granted will prevail. The power to define normality is not divided equally. A second observation relating to normality is that it changes over time. What used to be normal need no longer be so. From the perspective of citizenship, these two observations—of unequal power of definition and of change over time—force us to make normality a problem. Just as every speaker of Dutch is a carrier of language, so every citizen is a legitimate codefiner of normality. Normality can be adjusted by interventions from citizens and is, to them, not a decisive given. Because of the fact that the organizing power of normality lies to a great extent in its obviousness, normality cannot be problematized without encountering tensions.

There is not one morality, a kind of "natural" civic responsibility, which springs forth ready-made from society. We find instead multiple moralities, connected with the various practices citizens participate in. The citizens' task is to combine these in such a way that the reproduction of citizens is furthered and not hampered. There is no ready-made formula for succeeding in this task. Even when we limit ourselves to two conflicting sets of demands, namely those of citizenship and those of a particular office, there is no clear-cut priority for the one or the other. From the neorepublican point of view, neither citizenship nor the rules of office may be taken as absolute. Of course, in normal circumstances the rules of a particular office should usually get priority. If it were otherwise, that would mean that the office should be redesigned. When an office is reasonably well designed in a republic, we may assume that its demands usually will coincide or fit with those of citizenship.

However well designed, sometimes there are serious conflicts that cannot be resolved by a single formula. Here we need to practice (to learn by doing) the specific citizens' competence of organizing difference: judgment, coproduction with fellow citizens, and the courage to choose and stand up for your choice. This is no easy matter—not only because the right course of action is not obvious but also because the consequences for the person involved may be very unpleasant. Think of the fate of whistle-blowers in organizations, who however they may be admired in times when they courageously exposed some evil, so often ended up with their personal lives and their careers in shambles.

The demands of citizenship are *disturbing* not only because they demand a disruption of what counts as normalcy in the name of the normativity of citizenship but also because they may pose a really tragic choice. Tragic situations are such that whatever way one turns, something dear and of uncontested value will be sacrificed. Tragic choices are painful. We would like to avoid them. Where they are unavoidable, we usually entrust them not to individuals but to officials in robes, whose activities are circumscribed by rules and supported by rituals of office. It is therefore precisely in the fulfillment of particular public offices that citizens will be confronted with tragic choices, especially so when the demands of citizenship invite them to move beyond the safety provided by the rules and rituals of office. We also try to avoid tragic choice by rechristening the lesser of two evils as good. In real life, this deception does not work. The killing of one person to save ten other lives may be the thing to do, but it remains evil. This truth was captured by Saint Augustine of Hippo, who told early Christians that they had an obligation to serve the state, although by fulfilling it, they might commit more sins.

This chapter has shown that citizenship is at stake in the fulfillment of public office, and in what ways. It is precisely in addressing the problematic relations between the demands of citizenship and those of a particular office that occupants of those offices and citizens who have to deal with them show and learn what citizenship in the republic entails. It is there, among other places, that citizens are formed and citizenship is constituted. The idea of citizenship is a guideline for the fulfillment of office; a corrective for the "normal" demands of office; and a safety valve for revolutionary situations in which the constitutional relations between offices in the republic have been disrupted or have become unstable.

Part Three

□ □ □

How Citizens
Are Formed

SEVEN

□ □ □

Education

After having looked at what citizens do, at their practices of freedom, we now turn to how citizens are formed, to cultural reproduction and emancipation. Citizens do not come into the world all at once, in a fully mature state, but are formed through education and experience. The reproduction of citizens is primarily the business of adult members of society in their practice of freedom. But it is also a question of the admission to membership and the emancipation toward freedom of newcomers, of people in positions of quasi slavery, and of children who are being educated for entry into a particular culture and political regime. This chapter addresses one access route to citizenship: the education of children. Other ways along which citizens are formed, such as in immigration or in the discipline of performing a job, will be considered in subsequent chapters.

Complaints about contemporary education are common: It is inefficient and expensive, its outdated curricula and methods of teaching do not adequately prepare the brighter students for life in a postindustrial economy, while the less gifted or less privileged ones often leave school without having acquired basic skills of reading, writing, and calculating. Educational reform, of both institutions and curricula, is on the agenda.

Complaints about politics are heard just as often: Politicians are inept or corrupt, the political process is characterized by inertia and stagnation, ordinary citizens turn away from ordinary politics toward private enjoyment or political extremism. Political reconstruction, as in central Europe, the European Union, Italy, and Japan, is on the agenda.

There are likewise complaints about morality: Relativism and callousness are rampant, and there is a loss of social cohesion and community, of responsibility and civility. Moral regeneration is on the agenda.

Combined, the agendas of moral, political, and educational reform have stimulated an interest in education for citizenship (Pangle 1992; Steiner 1994; Gutman 1987; De Winter 1995). Would such education produce politically active and loyal citizens who cherish and respect moral values and norms, and who are competent and flexible enough to function in turbulent and high-tech markets? Before one can begin to answer such a question, one must consider what qualities of education are necessary to the effective practice of citizenship.

DANGEROUS QUESTIONS

These are dangerous questions. Why? In studies of citizenship, the turn toward education is always suspect, because it often disguises a failure to understand and improve citizen interaction among adults. Problems of citizenship concern issues that adults have to settle among themselves. The political process itself is the most important education for citizenship. The concern with education for citizenship is often fed by irresponsible, wishful thinking: If men were different, they would not have the problems they have—let us therefore make a new man. Such a transformation, if it has a place anywhere, belongs to the realms of religion and art. It should be kept out of politics, because there it usually results in indoctrination and murder. Thus, education and upbringing should not be used as means for solving problems of citizenship. They should provide access to citizenship such as it is—no more and no less.

The education of children should not be used to solve problems that adults have. However, it is an illusion to think that such misuses of education can be avoided by insisting on "neutral" schooling that focuses exclusively on reading, writing, calculating, and more advanced technical skills. In educational practice, inequality and dependency are unavoidable. Dealing with them, organizing difference and unequal vulnerability, is therefore equally unavoidable. When we recall that the organization of difference (in such a way that everyone has a respected place and voice) is what citizenship is about, then we see that citizenship is always at stake in educational practice, regardless of whether those involved know it. Students learn by how adults, particularly their teachers, deal with difference and dependence, by how they go about the tasks of heeding the weaker and inarticulate voices of members of a community and of fostering their competence. Education is unavoidably a practical exercise in citizenship.

A second reason why neutral schooling is not an option is that citizens do not grow spontaneously from the tree of civil society. Pruning—making choices of a political nature—is indispensable at many turns. Such choices are made by parents, teachers, and other persons involved in education. Their discretionary powers are constrained by the requirements of (access to) citizenship. Positively, educational practice should offer what is minimally required to provide (a reasonable chance of) access to a position of political equality; and negatively, while educating for whatever purposes, educators should not use means or engage in practices that run counter to the elementary demands of citizenship (no slavery in any form).

EDUCATION FOR CULTURE

Conceptions of what education entails vary. I do not consider them all here but only roughly indicate my own conception of education.

Education is a Lamarckian transmission of acquired characteristics of culture. People are vitally dependent on culture, they cannot do without it. For modern man to survive is a matter of "culture or nothing." Cultures are variable. One cannot acquire culture in general but only a particular culture. Acquiring a culture requires living in a context that is self-evidently given and within which meaning can emerge (Bruner 1990). Without context, there can be no meaning and no culture. Context is stabilized by institutions that to a large extent determine what and how we see, feel, and think. Institutions structure perception, valuation, and experience (Douglas 1992). In modern republics there are institutions that "produce" individuals. (Individual students, for instance, are required to write their *own* papers and to give their *own* answers, but these should nevertheless meet *institutional* requirements.) Individuals may forget their institutional embeddedness and come to think that "in the beginning was the individual." But such forgetfulness soon leads to the loss of their real individuality. When there is no acknowledged institutional hierarchy, there is also no order where the voice of the individual citizen can be heard and be effective. In order to flourish, individuality needs a context of institutional hierarchy. Although its place has become uncertain since the erstwhile hierarchy of educational institutions has become fragmented, school is still an important stabilizer and transmitter of culture—to be more precise, of the culture of individuality.

Let us now consider the relations of education, thus conceived, with various conceptions of citizenship. The conception of the citizen as an individual calculator and holder of rights will emphasize aspects of education such as the acquisition of individual skills of a technical/instrumental nature and a sound understanding of personal interest based on calculation and personal choice. The communitarian will emphasize the importance of morality and common values. The republican will foster a readiness for public service and political participation. And what will neorepublicans say? Obviously, they will emphasize aspects of education that involve the organization of difference. The elaboration of this point of view is the main task of this chapter. The other conceptions of citizenship and their view of education serve as contrasting background for this exploration.

EDUCATORS AS EXEMPLARY CITIZENS

What orientation does citizenship provide in the practice of education? What view on education do neorepublicans hold? How will they act as participants in educational practices?

Neorepublicans conceive of citizenship and education as two distinct practices in their own right. They do not formulate requirements of citizenship and then deductively design an education that serves these. Combining, and where necessary choosing between, requirements of these two practices is precisely the difficult task that citizens who are involved in education must undertake. This requires judgment, which cannot be avoided by applying a theoretical formula or by defining one practice as subordinate to the other.

Teachers are the primary addressees of the requirements of citizenship. They are the fully adult citizens who must practice their citizenship in the educational situation. They are both citizens and educators, and the way in which they combine these offices should offer their pupils instructive examples of the exercise of citizenship.

Education for living in a plural society is necessarily political. If the core virtue or competence of citizenship is the organization of plurality, then such education is by its very nature education for citizenship. Thus, all education, and not only the explicit teachings about citizenship in civics courses, is a formative exercise in ruling and being ruled. (What is missing is the alternation between positions of ruler and ruled. I consider this difficulty later on.) The people who have been brought together in the classroom learn to transform their community of fate into an association in which there is a place and voice for each and every member. In order to achieve this, they have to organize their differences. What is being demonstrated and learned is not primarily that plurality should be organized, but rather *how* this might be done—a repertoire of moves, judgments about where to apply them, and judgments about how this repertoire fits with that of others. When successful, such an organization of plurality may engender as by-products loyalty and a sense of identity as a community member. Education that aims directly at such outcomes will not be effective. It will fail to produce the experiences and competences in which loyalty and identity are grounded.

Neorepublican citizens will focus on issues *in* educational situations that require and exemplify citizen competence: how to transform violent disputes into verbal ones, how to organize debate and exchange between different points of view, how to relate these to decisionmaking and authority. They will view educational situations as "fractals" of politics—at least up to a point, because education resembles politics in some respects but differs from it in crucial others. Education offers young people, precisely because they lack the competence of full, adult citizens, a protected area where they can learn, experiment, fail, and try themselves out in relative safety. They are protected from some consequences and implications that obtain in adult life for as long as they are thought to lack resources and insight to deal with them. They may be told about the adult world and its dealings without being directly exposed to it. They learn about politics taking place over there, about what is expected from adult citizens—that is, from people that they are going to be but are not yet.

From the point of view of citizenship, such teachings about the world out there harbor two dangers. Pupils may come to think that citizenship is not their affair and fail to appreciate how educational experiences mold their civic competence. And teachers may come to think that they may mold pupils to become a better or different kind of citizen. From a neorepublican point of view, citizenship is at stake in all practices and institutions of social life—in nursing homes, in asylums, in the secret service, and in education. Citizenship is one principle that orders and guides such activities. It is a reserve circuit for ambiguous and turbulent situations, in which it helps us choose a course of action that serves the reproduction or restoration of citizenship for all members of a community of fate. Citizenship works as a guiding principle in situations like that of education, in which people are half free, neither completely autonomous nor pure slaves. The freedom of citizens is not a given possession but appears *in* the movement from dependence toward autonomy. If one accepts this point of view, then education, with its task of guiding dependent pupils toward the competences of adults, is an experience more suited to modeling, building, and practicing citizenship than it might at first appear.

What is it that participants learn in educational situations that are guided by considerations of citizenship? They acquire social competences and communicative skills. They learn how actions are related to outcomes, both morally and sociologically. They are informed about nonobvious social mechanisms such as the dilemma of the commons, oligarchization, and private vices and public benefits, and the conditions under which these obtain. They are taught about, and on a small scale participate in, institutions for dealing with difference, such as committees, elections, representative bodies, judges and juries, and all offices with authority. Thus, it is hoped, they will acquire the tools for deliberative judgment and learn to avoid the extremes of arbitrary subjectivity and dogmatic loyalty.

THE PROBLEM OF RIPENESS AND OTHER DILEMMAS

Thus, the neorepublican conception of citizenship provides orientation and guidance in some educational matters. There is, however, a major educational dilemma that remains beyond its reach, namely the problem of ripeness. Particular elements of human knowledge and learning should not be offered to children before they are ready for them. Readiness is supposed to depend on earlier learning and development. Every educator has some notion of stages of development and of the position his pupils occupy in it. In most theories of development, skipping a stage is supposed to be detrimental. Plato (*Politeia* VIII:537–540) thought that to engage in dialectic would be destructive for people under thirty. Parents from the 1960s, who treated their children as adults, now often acknowledge that as a result their offspring have refused to grow up, remaining stuck in the stage of development that was denied them.

Ripeness constitutes a major dilemma for educators, including those who want to guide their pupils toward citizenship. Citizenship requires alternation between ruling and being ruled, dealing with a plurality of moral convictions and lifestyles, and thinking critically about things that are normally taken for granted. But before one can meaningfully engage in such activities, one must have experienced what it is to be ruled, have acquired primary moral convictions (a mother-morality like a mother tongue), and been provided with a safe and "natural" context within which events and actions can acquire meaning (without a context, there can be no meaning). The requirements of authority, toleration, and criticism that obtain between citizens have a secondary or metacharacter. They presuppose the prior existence and grounding of the primary attitudes and commitments that they reorganize. If these are insufficiently grounded, as they are in the earlier stages of development, then exposure to the secondary requirements of citizenship will destroy the primary materials and commitments that they are supposed to modify and organize. Children will slip into premature relativism or into arbitrary dogmatism—both attitudes that are inimical to the commitments of citizenship. Children who are denied the right to be children cannot grow up.

Therefore, the full requirements and concomitant rights of citizenship should not be visited upon children from the start. Their applicability depends on a judgment about ripeness. This judgment in turn depends on the theory about development that the educator has and on his guess about the stage of development that the pupil is presently in. On the basis of such guesses, pupils are brought together in classes and treated accordingly. Access to citizenship through education is heavily dependent on judgments and theories of educators. These, we expect, will be shot through with prejudice. The usual way to combat prejudice, however, cannot be traveled here. Pupils who are prematurely required to decide as fully critical citizens are thereby denied access to full citizenship. Effective citizen criticism of educational theories and judgments, therefore, must be largely indirect. It will come from parents and other representatives of the pupils, and it will usually be of a general nature and will not interfere with actual educational situations. Such interference is indicated only in clear cases of repression and discrimination, that is, of education for, or in a spirit of, slavery.

Apart from ripeness, there are several other educational dilemmas that remain problematic for neorepublican educators, albeit less so than for those who adhere to earlier conceptions of citizenship. In those earlier visions, consensus and a general attitude of loyalty, discipline, and equality were final values, citizen qualities that pupils were supposed to acquire. In the neorepublican vision, with its emphasis on the organization of plurality, these are not central ingredients of full citizenship. They are indispensable supports at some stages of education on the road toward citizenship, but they are not core requirements of full citizenship. At the stage of full citizenship, they are relativized, criticized, and modified.

Let us illustrate this with regard to consensus. In many theories, consensus is conceived as a necessary condition for citizens acting together in peace. This assumption was criticized in Chapter 4, where I argued that consensus is not a condition but a problem that citizens have to work on. Consensus is not a precondition but rather the desired outcome of citizen activities. Thus, in the classroom, the point of citizen education will not be to provide a unity of values and meanings that will obtain once and for all, but to acquire competence in dealing with difference in such a way that consensus is the outcome.

Similar arguments apply to dilemmas of loyalty, discipline, and equality in education. Loyalty, discipline, and equality are neither general values nor necessary conditions of neorepublican citizenship. The specific outcomes that citizen activities strive for are not loyalty in general but loyalty to the republic; not general obedience but the discipline to obey citizens who fulfill the office of ruling; not social equality but access for all to a position of political equality. Citizenship involves both the acceptance of rules of order and the freedom to criticize and change the rules. If citizens are to have an effective voice, there must be a hierarchy, an established and respected order within which their voices can be heard and heeded. Without such a hierarchy, no voice can be heard. Like other voices, the voice of the citizen needs an order within which it can be heard and make sense. What is special about a republic is that this voice may rightfully contest and aim to modify the very hierarchy on which it depends. But when it completely forgets this dependence, then it will soon cease to be heard. When the individual forgets the institutional supports of his own "independence," he will soon lose his autonomy.

FRAGMENTATION AND THE AVOIDANCE OF EXPERIENCE

In our considerations up till now, we have presupposed protected educational situations of school and family. However, in contemporary societies, these are no longer the oligopolistic, total institutions that they once might have been. Many educational experiences take place outside them. Children are consumers, go to discos, travel abroad, learn to make bombs from computer bulletin boards, watch television, and enjoy commercials. This shift has two consequences. First, school and family have become organizations among others. Educators have to organize their place among others. In families, the question "When do we eat together?" frequently arises. Second, school and family have ceased to be self-evident settings that compel children to have experiences and learn from them. In contemporary societies, pupils have many escapes that allow them to avoid unpleasant experiences. Thus, they can avoid unhappiness, pain, and cruelty, but by the same token also the learning that comes with real experience.

Does their wider access to the school of real life not compensate for this paucity of experience and learning in the classroom and the family? Did not Mandela, Havel, and Dostoyevsky learn what they became famous for in the school of real life? Yes, but many young people cannot profit from the school of real life in this way. They have ample choice—that is, opportunity for escape from experience that leads to learning. And where they have little choice—such as among ten-year-old boys in South Chicago, who have a choice between dying or becoming a gang member—the learning is so one-sided as to disable them for citizenship.

Experience—as with the child who burns his or her hand on the stove—is necessary for learning. The more choice, the more escape from experience and the less learning. Education in family and school provided a protected environment for learning. Certain experiences, and therefore some kinds of learning, were excluded. But a plural consumer's society also offers ample opportunities for escape from experience and learning: A great deal of information is available, but the self-evident context that binds people and within which information acquires meaning is missing. The scarcity of context leads to a scarcity (thinness) of meaning and experience, and this in turn to poor or superficial learning. This, it seems to me, is the kernel of truth in the otherwise misplaced calls for more discipline and morality in the classroom.

WHO EDUCATES THE EDUCATOR?

Neorepublican educators will acknowledge the indispensability of a primary mother-morality for younger children. With older children, they will continue to emphasize the importance of morality, of having values. Without values (things that we hold dear), painful experience, perception, and valuation can hardly develop. But neorepublican educators will reject the equation between moral education and education for citizenship. With regard to moralities, citizenship has a metaposition—not higher, but of a *different* order. Citizenship concerns conflicting moralities, the organization of a diversity of moral convictions, both between persons and between roles or offices that one person fulfills. After freedom of religion, freedom of morality became an established principle. Not because, as some have thought, religion or morality have become less important, but because they are so central that we must do our utmost to learn to organize their differences peacefully. This cannot be done by imposing, or presupposing, a unity or consensus. Unity has to be created by the differing parties themselves. The institutions of the republic provide a setting and means for citizens to do this. Educational institutions should facilitate access to this institutional reality, without, however, undermining their own specific institutional character.

It is to be expected that educators will sometimes fail in this task. They may harm pupils through cruelty or out of laziness. But even good intentions are insufficient to prevent real harm from education. Educators may withhold precisely what pupils need to learn and grow up. Like all other approaches to citizenship and education, neorepublicanism has to consider what to do when things go wrong, when recommendations do not work or are not implemented as expected. An approach to education and citizenship should not only be judged on its bright side, but also on its darker aspects, on how it limits damage when things go wrong. Who will control and educate the educator?

Obviously, a theory of neorepublican citizenship cannot answer this eternally crucial question once and for all. But it is in a somewhat better position than its rival theories to tackle it for two reasons: first, because of its limited conception of citizenship as (access to) *political* equality, and second, because of the broad applicability of this notion of citizenship as a reserve circuit for emergencies in all practices of life, including those of education. Reproduction of citizens is an important value in the politics of education at all levels, from classroom to parliament.

Designing and running a program of preparation for citizenship is a thorny and messy affair, both in theory and in practice. The skills that the exercise of citizenship requires are not given by nature but acquired in the practice of a particular culture and in explicit instruction and learning. What form might the trajectory of access to citizenship take? Obviously, the freedoms of citizenship cannot fully apply there, because those involved (are supposed to) lack the requisite competence. The introductory trajectory therefore will be characterized by constraints (mixtures of discipline, force, and persuasion) that are forbidden in the end state to which it is supposed to lead—citizenship.

The trajectory toward citizenship has uncivic traits. How long may prospective citizens be kept in it, and what examination hurdles may be posed at the end of it? What about requirements that exceed, or deviate from, those that full citizens actually meet? And what in fact should be taught? Such questions must be answered in a coherent way if children are to get what (we think) they need: real education—which is different from learning the joys of the consumer society and the bitterness of political conflict. The answers need not be the same across the board; but within individual educational institutions and trajectories, coherence is imperative, because trust and training require stability and firmness. At the same time, we know that since education is unavoidably cultural, such "local" coherence can be contested outside the classroom and particular educational institutions. Little is known about the social and cultural conditions of citizenship, which makes any attempt to design a learning program for access to citizenship extremely hazardous.

EIGHT

□   □   □

Admission
and Exclusion

When we turn from education of children of citizen-parents to the admission of strangers, we must not only address the program of preparation for citizenship itself but also the decision about whether people are eventually to be admitted to full citizenship. Because citizenship, like having a home, is unavoidably local and culturally specific, not all the people in the world can be admitted to it at the same time. What principle of selection may citizens use? This is not a trivial matter, since by selecting they draw the contours of their community of fate. They define the set of people to whom they are related—by chance, fate, history, or choice—in ways that are so binding or pressing that they deserve to be transformed into the equality that obtains between citizens.

The admission decision not only defines the community of those who deserve to relate as citizens but also excludes the "undeserving"—those whom citizens consider their enemies, or those to whom citizens are indifferent or consider themselves only tenuously and superficially related. Cozy inside, cold outside: Exclusion is the dark side of noble notions of citizenship. It is difficult to justify exclusion, departing from premises of equality and freedom for all. The opposite of citizenship is slavery and dictatorship. Once one acknowledges that the price of citizenship for some is slavery and unfreedom for others, the joys of citizenship become tainted. Some have, as a consequence, shifted their focus from the local to the global. They aim for world citizenship, or for a world order in which local citizenship is accessible to all, or for transnational membership and rights in international migration (Bauböck 1994; Soysal 1994). The trouble with such laudable efforts to secure citizenship for all, everywhere, is that they tend to make citizenship lose its distinctiveness and cutting edge.

Wisdom and effectiveness lie somewhere between overreaching and exclusiveness, but no one knows exactly where.

The first two sections of this chapter consider questions of admission as they arise in normative argument and practical policies. A third and final section briefly treats forms of exclusion from citizenship. Exclusion is often considered the mirror image of admission, on the assumption that the criteria for admission are identical with those for exclusion. Why, then, a special section on exclusion? Because the mirror image applies only to the exclusion of those who never were citizens of the particular polity in question. Exclusion, partial or total, of those who are, or once were, citizens is an entirely different matter, a matter that should not be regulated by rules concerning the admission of newcomers. Traitors, collaborators, crazies, and crooks may be considered for exclusion, but not on the grounds that they would not qualify for admission. Moreover, there are good grounds for maintaining that expulsion from citizenship, once it is obtained, is never justified.

Obviously, there are also good reasons for treating admission and exclusion in one chapter. Not only do both show, sometimes painfully, what it is to be or not to be a citizen of this particular polity, but they also in some situations unavoidably touch upon each other in uneasy ways. Why should this be so? Admission aims at inclusion of people as equal citizens. In order to secure such inclusion, such access to a position of political equality, it is at times necessary to compartmentalize, to make distinctions between categories of people who do and who presently do not (yet) have the qualities minimally required for the exercise of citizenship. Newcomers are seldom immediately admitted. Most have to go through various procedures and "inspections" before the last barriers to full citizenship are lifted. During these procedures, they therefore are excluded from citizenship. We encounter a similar compartmentalization and exclusion with children, demented people, prisoners, and members of minorities with no reasonable access to the politics of citizens, all of whom need special treatment, different from what obtains between ordinary citizens, precisely because they lack the minimum qualities that the exercise of citizenship requires. The danger of such compartmentalization, both with newcomers and with people who for the time being cannot function "normally," is semipermanent inequality and hierarchy, creeping exclusion under the guise of moving toward emancipation. Just as in cases of citizenship and other, supposedly "higher" or special offices (considered in Chapter 6), here, with persons who supposedly are "below" the minimum requirements of citizenship, access to citizenship also is a governing value. The difference is that here it is not one value among others but rather the value that is to be maximized. This is so because the position of people who are treated differently has traits that are the very opposite of citizenship.

CLAIMS FOR ADMISSION AND GROUNDS FOR REFUSAL

There are many claims that individuals make in order to be admitted as new citizens of a particular republic. From a neorepublican point of view, the prima facie acceptable claims can be arranged in three categories. The first principle is mutual consent between the aspiring citizen and the republic. The second principle is that of a community of fate. It bases the claim of admission on the fact that those aspiring to citizenship are already subjected to the power of the state of which they wish to become a member. The third principle is negative: The prospective citizen's claim is valid because he or she has no access to any other citizenship in the world, and citizenship somewhere should be available to everyone. To refuse such a person citizenship would be to make the person stateless, effectively denying him or her citizenship in this world.

The first principle, mutual consent, seems simple and straightforward: What can be wrong, when both parties agree? But other parties might disagree: Third parties might feel deprived of a job that they might have gotten if the newcomer had not been let in. Those who are not admitted might feel unfairly deprived because others were. And why should German scientists who had worked for their fatherland during World War II be allowed to become U.S. citizens after the war, while homeless orphans had to make their lives in the devastated country that the new U.S. citizens had left behind? Notwithstanding these difficulties in its practical application, the principle itself is unobjectionable from a neorepublican perspective. Choice and freedom are central values of the republic. When citizens choose to receive new members, that is enough reason to admit them.

More problematic is the second principle, that people have a claim to become citizens if in their daily life and its medium-term prospects they cannot avoid being subjected to the state's power. This principle is problematic because it is based on the contested notion of a community of fate. Such a community obtains when people are connected in ways they cannot avoid—bodily (or in symbolic space that works as directly as bodily presence) and also systematically (air-polluting factories do not distinguish between citizens and aliens). However, people disagree in their views of what may be avoided, both empirically and normatively. Some insist on systematic connections that others cannot see or prefer to ignore because they cannot find a way to adequately deal with them. A community of fate obtains when people cannot avoid each other without depriving themselves of what is essential for their way of life. But opinions as to what is essential differ. And what if not avoiding each other also destroys your way of life? Like the first principle, the second is unobjectionable from a neorepublican point of view; but its application in practice is much riddled with problems and conflicts. This is so because defining the contours of a community of fate is precisely what political conflict is often about.

The third principle on which claims of access to citizenship are based is weakest from a neorepublican point of view, because it lies beyond the horizon and powers of the republic. The requirement that there be a republic with decent citizenship for every person in the world is situated at the world level, whereas effective citizenship, as we have known it until now, is local. When applied at the world level, beyond the effective reach of the republic, citizenship loses its cutting edge. It becomes an ideal that is insufficiently fed and realized by institutions. Efforts to develop a world citizenship have foundered on the inherently local character of citizenship. The world scene, the so-called international society, is at best a place for what Walzer (1994) calls thin, or minimalist moral argument. Thick moral arguments, which obtain within the sphere of the domestic republic and its direct environment, are ineffectual and misunderstood when used at the world level.

The third principle is accepted in the abstract but in fact is applied by republics only insofar as it can be reconstructed as a subspecies of the second principle—that is, when something of a special relationship, resembling a community of fate, obtains between the aspiring citizen and the particular republic. The "specialness" may appear quite thin—it may consist in the fact that this republic happened to be the first to which political refugees fled—but it may quickly become strengthened by "thick" arguments from countries that refuse refugees on the grounds that they first arrived in a neighboring republic. Obviously, neorepublicans cannot disagree with the view that citizenship in a republic should be available to all persons in the world; but they can act only locally, not globally, to effect this principle, and only for some individuals (to whom they are connected in local and particular ways), and not for others.

Claims for admission that are prima facie acceptable need not always be decisive. Although the republic is obliged to consider them seriously, it nevertheless may refuse candidates because they do not meet the requirements of citizenship or because there is no room for them. What do these grounds for refusing admission involve, and are they valid? Four conditions of acceptance are often brought forward: (a) general citizen competence, (b) competence to act as a member of this particular polity, (c) acceptance of local culture, and (d) enough room for the new citizen.

Requirement (a) is rather obvious. Those who want to be citizens must be capable of dialogic performance. They must, within limits, be ready to argue with other citizens, to talk and listen to them, and to form judgments on the basis of such dialogue. They must also be able and willing to make their actions conform to their words—at least, within limits.

Requirement (b) concerns a working knowledge of and respect for the political ways of life of the republic, and for its legal and political institutions for dealing with conflicts. In order to participate in the life of this polity, prospective citizens must understand at least one of its languages for public communication and must respect its laws, particularly its laws for changing laws. Once they have become citizens, they may engage in political activity to change the political culture; but as newcomers, they can gain entrance only by accepting that culture. This requirement, as obvious as it may seem at first sight, may pose serious problems for newcomers when the requirements of the prevailing political culture conflict with some of their own "deep" beliefs. In Chapter 5, we considered how the republic may accommodate "deep" group differences that arise among its own citizens. It should do all it can, provided it does not put the continuation of the republic itself, or the reproduction of citizens, at risk. The same conclusion holds with regard to newcomers who have a prima facie claim to admittance as citizens.

The third requirement, that aspiring citizens accept the local culture (whether it is called national, traditional, or whatever), is squarely rejected by neorepublicans. Citizenship concerns acceptance of and competence in ways of dealing with cultural and social differences, not acceptance of one style of life that happens to be dominant or fashionable. On this point, neorepublicans differ sharply with those who hold communitarian views on citizenship.

The fourth requirement, which provides grounds for refusing citizens with a prima facie acceptable claim to entry, because the country is "full," is always suspect, but unlike the third requirement, is not necessarily invalid. Even within a given community of fate, there may not be a permanent place for every member: Remember, for instance, that during the Allied landing in Normandy in 1944, some had to go first and to die. A republic may be full, or rather "overfilled," in the sense that it cannot survive without denying a place to some persons.

Ground (c) is to be rejected out of hand. The other grounds are valid in principle, but their application demands situational judgment. They are not equally compelling in all situations. When entry is claimed on the basis of mutual consent, as for instance with a valued soccer player, manager, or scientist, refusal may be based on (a), (b), or (d). When entry claims are based on a community of fate, on de facto subjection to the state's power, then a lack of general and specific citizen competence—(a) and (b)—are grounds for refusal, but not the argument that there is no room for newcomers (d). In the case of admission claims based on the fact that there is no other place in the world for the prospective citizen, on the contrary, the argument of no room is in principle valid (the republic cannot receive the entire world population as members), while the compelling force of arguments of citizen competence is much weaker than in other situations considered here. The first concern is to secure a place for this person as a citizen, not how well he or she may exercise citizenship in the future.

ADMISSION POLICIES AND PRACTICES

These are neorepublican principles. What of practice? Do the principles provide orientation and correction there, or are practical policies so different that principles have no grip on them—that is, on those who make and implement policies?

In practice, in Europe and the United States, newcomers and new applicants for citizenship are seen as problems, not as assets. The efforts of the receiving polity are directed toward keeping out as many as possible and letting in only the most deserving. There are many rules and schemes for separating the deserving from the undeserving applicants. There are also schemes for monitoring and controlling the flow of migration. Both efforts are notoriously ineffective. One explanation (among many) for this failure is that the rules and practices for separating deserving from undeserving applicants for citizenship demand investments of time and judgment that are incompatible with the quick-and-dirty decisionmaking required to control the collective flow of migration.

The countries of the European Union are placing an increasing emphasis on stricter policies of admission to and expulsion from their territories. The common ingredients of these policies are quick decisionmaking, no economic refugees, and international coordination. Quick decisionmaking is thought necessary in order to avoid de facto settlement on the territory. Economic refugees should not take the places reserved for "real" (i.e., political) refugees. International coordination is needed to prevent countries thought to be overly generous from being overwhelmed (they should be brought into line); to achieve a reasonable distribution of refugees over west European countries; and to repair "leaks" in the control system (for instance, as in Italy or at the Amsterdam airport).

Such policies meet with considerable difficulties. Quick decisionmaking on matters of such importance is callousness when information is scarce and unreliable, when barriers of language and culture are considerable, and when there is no reasonable period during which the partners involved can try each other out. What is the difference between economic and political refugees? Politics and economics, as we know, hang together. The only sure proof of being a political refugee seems to be that one should have died but was saved by an inexplicable miracle. International coordination is a shadowy affair. Conferences among government ministers and civil servants are not public, and only selected results are announced. Spin management about the porousness of various west European countries' borders or about the fragility of a common European Union admissions policy is a difficult affair, particularly if one wants to impress persons in faraway countries who are struggling for survival.

Governments have made strong efforts to speed up the decisionmaking process about individual admissions. Their ideal is the "airport decision"—that is, deciding about entry or expulsion as close as possible to the time and place of arrival of the newcomers. These government efforts are notoriously unsuccessful and unjust in their outcomes. Gaining entry becomes a lottery, in which some win and others lose. Quick decisionmaking is often based on insufficient or false information and sometimes on bribery. Officials deciding about entry always exercise their own discretion, however many rules and instructions there may be. Their judgment may be arbitrary and must therefore be open to challenge before a judge. Otherwise the officials would exercise tyranny (arbitrary power unchecked by law) over the entrants. Legal procedures, however, take time. And the longer applicants stay in the country, the better are their chances of staying permanently. The legal procedure itself creates some kind of community of fate. It is notoriously difficult to remove applicants whose legal appeals have finally come to naught from the territory of the polity.

Many European countries offer practically no official immigration possibilities. People can only enter as political refugees or as family members of people who are already legally resident in the country. Those who wish to come to the country and who would surely take the route of immigration if it were open, have no choice but to enter illegally or in the capacity of a helpless refugee or family member. These are not promising tickets with which to start one's voyage as a new member of the republic. Having to behave as a helpless person is not a good way to start out as an autonomous citizen.

These questions of admission to citizenship arise not only at the borders of the polity. There are many noncitizens who have been living inside the borders of the republic. Whether their stay has been legal or not, such an extended period of living on the same territory constitutes a community of fate and therefore a claim to be recognized as citizens. Should these resident aliens have a right to acquire citizenship or even be "obliged to choose" citizenship? Should they live according to the habits and the prevailing culture of the land? From a neorepublican point of view, the first question should in principle be answered affirmatively. Allowing second-class membership to be a permanent or terminal station in the lives of some members of a community of fate would violate the demands of political equality in the republic. From a neorepublican point of view, long-term residents may be required to accept citizenship, but not on condition that they give up their "old" citizenship. Multiple citizenship is quite acceptable for neorepublicans as long as it is based on a connectedness that is strong enough to be classified as a community of fate. The requirement that newcomers integrate into the culture of their new country is increasingly voiced, these days: Children should not show their religious allegiance at school by how they are dressed; newcomers should get acquainted with local customs and Christian values. All such requirements to conform are mistaken from a neorepublican point of view. Multicultural citizenship, and not one dominant monoculture, is the norm. What should be accepted by all, however, are political rules for organizing cultural differences. For example, Muslim girls should be free to wear head scarves in school, but they should not be obliged to do so against their will.

We began this inquiry by stating some rules and principles that from a neorepublican point of view would be appropriate as guides regulating admission to citizenship. We then briefly considered admission practices and saw that they tell an entirely different story. The rules and principles have very little real influence and provide little guidance for practical problems. We have to conclude that admission of adults to citizenship remains a rather arbitrary affair from a neorepublican perspective. This perspective works fully and well, inside the republic, but not outside (and around) the borders of the republic. Does this indicate a fatal failure of neorepublican theory? No, because a theory of citizenship is not to be taken as a full-fledged theory of justice. The scope of citizenship is limited and local. In our globalizing and migrating world, insisting on the value of citizenship does not prevent tragic conflicts between the demands of global justice and local citizenship. When the decision in such tragic dilemmas is left with officials/citizens of a particular polity, they may decide myopically and easily—too easily from the point of view of justice—in favor of the inside perspective.

Some have tried to remedy this unpalatable state of affairs by developing notions of world citizenship, transnational membership, and rights in migration (Bauböck 1994; Soysal 1994). Such ideal schemes remain ineffective as long as they are not fed by firmly established institutions. There are efforts to establish such institutions, as in the case of the Maastricht treaty on citizenship of the European Union, or the Schengen agreements among a number of countries to abolish their mutual border controls; but they run again and again into practical difficulties and outright obstruction by the very national authorities who signed the agreements.

World citizenship is a reality for an international elite of businessmen, stars, scientists, and others who travel freely around the world and have access to the cosmopolis of communication, finance, and leisure. From a neorepublican perspective, this is not citizenship. Although neorepublicanism does not require social equality, it does require political equality—that is, access to political control of the real centers of decisionmaking for all, not just for the privileged few.

EXCLUSION OF CITIZENS

In this section, we look at exclusion from citizenship that is not simply the result of a refusal of admission of newcomers but that involves people who are, or at any time have been, citizens of the polity in question. Three forms of such exclusion may be distinguished: elimination or expulsion; second-class citizenship; and strong distinctions between "ordinary" citizens and "special" people, such as kings, business leaders, and other elites. We consider these in turn.

Straightforward exclusion occurs when citizenship is taken away and people are removed from the territory, put to death, or forcibly detained without legal protection. Exclusion also obtains when citizenship is not officially taken away but is nonetheless unavailable for all practical purposes. Examples are people who live in "no go" areas, where the state provides no legal protection (certain parts of big cities, or activities under mafia protection), or people who are excluded de facto from politics because of their convictions (communists in the United States during the Cold War, Muslim fundamentalists in present-day Algeria, and people everywhere who refuse to join in the swelling chorus of nationalist "consensus"). Such unofficial exclusion may be total or partial. An example of this last category is the special treatment of hard-core criminals as distinct from ordinary trespassers against the law. Criminals who have been labeled hard-core offenders are routinely denied certain protections of due process, even when the text of the law does not explicitly allow for such distinctions. Such cases of unofficial and partial exclusion from citizenship shade off into the second form of exclusion that we have distinguished, namely, second-class citizenship.

Second-class citizenship may be involuntary, as in the case of demented, unemployed, or homeless people, or more or less chosen, as with isolates, chaotics, and addicts. In the first category, the question is how far to go in meting out special compensatory treatment in order to secure the maximum of access to citizenship that is obtainable under those circumstances. Some compartmentalization and compensation are indicated, but how much is enough, where should the line be drawn, and what should we do when no amount of compensation is enough to actually compensate? With the second category of people, who more or less voluntarily have exited from full citizenship, the troubling question is to what extent they may be forced to reintegrate. This becomes all the more troubling when their original choice to exit may have been free in some sense, but when in their present situation their capacity to choose has been lost and reentry is not an option that they can take and implement on their own, without compensation and help. Think, for instance, of drug addicts and of the question of forced treatment and special provisions to "reintegrate" them into the working population.

A third form of exclusion is practiced by those who because of their special functions or qualities, place themselves above or apart from so-called ordinary citizens. (It is also practiced by ordinary citizens who defer to this classification.) This form of exclusion is widespread in modern meritocratic societies. It is wrong. In Chapter 6, I argued that citizenship does not stop where special offices like those of minister, judge, or chief executive officer are assumed, but is on the contrary indispensable to keeping the execution of such offices connected to the way we have decided to live together—as citizens who rule each other. If being an ordinary citizen is conceived of as being without special powers, offices, or talents (as being a residual category in a meritocratic society), and if occupying an office and having special powers are taken as signs that one has escaped from being a "mere" citizen, then citizenship will remain powerless. Such a view is mistaken, because it in fact defines citizens in such a way that they must remain powerless. Inasmuch as "ordinary" citizens acquire special powers, they cease to be "ordinary" citizens. The only general power that they have is that of voting in elections, which remains futile as long as its outcomes cannot be translated into special powers and decisions. Citizenship is as much a question of ordinary people as of special people who exercise special powers. It is precisely in the confrontation and uneasy (at times, even tragic) combination of these that citizenship is needed as a guiding value. It is precisely there that it develops a cutting edge and that people (painfully or with pleasure) learn what it takes (in real cost) to be a citizen.

The second form of exclusion, second-class citizenship, is equally wrong in principle but more difficult to appreciate and avoid in practice. People are not obliged to be citizens day and night; self-exclusion is permitted—but not on a permanent basis or in cases where the return to actual citizenship becomes impossible. Differentiating between people in order to secure or restore their access to citizenship is required; but an overemphasis on emancipation of groups of people may in fact exclude them more permanently. Respect for multiple loyalties is a requirement of citizenship in plural societies. But when this leads to such events as Moroccan women in The Netherlands leaving the police force because their "own" people threatened them or their relatives with violence unless the female officers provided "special" treatment, then something has gone terribly wrong.

The first form of exclusion from citizenship, expulsion or elimination, is certainly no longer a defensible option after World War II and the horrible experiences of persons deprived of the elementary protections of citizenship. All human beings have a right to citizenship in some polity, somewhere. In reality, many cannot realize this right. The least that citizens from polities that consider themselves civilized can do is to refrain from adding to those "many" by depriving their own cocitizens of their citizenship status. When citizens "misbehave," the only legitimate option is to temporarily compartmentalize them, to give them special treatment, always with a view toward restoring their access to full citizenship.

Thus, admission and exclusion are intertwined and belong together; but they are not each other's mirror image. Both are about who is in and who is not. Both define what it is to be a citizen of this polity and what the contours are of the community of fate that this polity considers itself responsible for, that it wants to take care of and to civilize. But admission and exclusion do not obey the same logic and rules, because the latter concerns citizens and the first concerns those who wish to become but are not yet citizens. Here, also, being a citizen does make a difference.

NINE

□ □ □

Work and Third Age Citizens

Many modern studies have established a correlation between work and civic participation. Those who have paid work participate more, and more responsibly. Such findings feed the thought that if more people had a job, the vitality of citizenship would be enhanced. Jobs discipline and activate people. For many policymakers in post-1989 democracies, this close connection between work and being a good citizen is so obvious as to need no argument—and certainly not an argument with long-dead people from the society in which the idea of citizenship was first articulated. Ancient Greeks saw work not as activating but as an impediment to citizenship. Those who had to work had no time for politics. Political activity was reserved for those who were free from the burden of work.

FROM PROPERTY TO SOCIAL RIGHTS

Until a hundred years ago, owning property, rather than having a job, was considered a primary condition for citizenship. Property, especially landed property, was supposed to give people a stake in the community, which, in turn, increased the likelihood of their exercising sound judgment and showing loyal attitudes. Ownership, as indicated by the adage "my home is my castle," also was seen as a sanctuary from which citizens could say "no" to people in authority. The presence of the key elements of citizenship—judgment, loyalty, autonomy, and not being a slave at the mercy of the power of the rulers—was thought to be closely related to ownership.

This idea deserves criticism not only because it excludes so many people from citizenship but also because it risks making a condition of citizenship—property—into its core. Thus, citizen action in the republic would become purely a means to ensure private property. From being a condition of citizenship, property would become its goal and point. Thereby, citizenship would lose much of its significance and appeal.

Later, the set of citizens was enlarged to include workers who do not own property but have an income from their work. In order to give this income a stability comparable to that provided by property, functional equivalents of ownership were created in the form of collective insurance that provided a substitute income in situations of unemployment, sickness, disability, and old age. Thereby even nonowners, as long as they were insured, could become wealthy in a sense: The operator of an automobile who has liability insurance might be "good for" half a million; the 65-year-old, for forty years of pension benefits; and the injured employee, for years of disability payments. Or think of the movie theme of the poor wretch who swindles his life insurance company by faking his own death, so as to provide his family with what he feels they have long deserved.

This wish to offer the noninsured also the elementary privileges of ownership—a wish that is based on considerations of social justice—was not only harbored by swindlers. Social assistance to citizens who did not own property and could not be sufficiently insured has been realized in various ways: by incorporating solidarity elements into social insurance schemes (which were originally based on pure equivalence, the allowance being a function of premium and risk); by extending the group of persons entitled to allowances from insurance; and by specific and general support provided by the state to the noninsured in the form of social help. Relief for the poor was reinterpreted as a right to benefits for those citizens who for whatever reason had no access to stable employment and the social insurance associated with it. Given this development, social insurance became less a set of special rights of workers and more a structure of rights that all citizens, and not only those who happened to have a job, (should) have. The fact that those rights were tied to having work was increasingly seen as a historical accident, as having to do with the way in which they were first established but not with what they essentially are.

With regard to citizenship, this development was theorized in the work of T. H. Marshall (1950), who argued that after a long struggle, socioeconomic rights were finally also becoming part of citizenship. This extension of the notion of citizenship was accepted without much criticism for a fairly long period. Some debate occurred on the question of whether social justice legitimizes the state's enforcement of solidarity. Yet, the majority of people who answered this question in the affirmative subsequently endorsed Marshall's extension of the notion of citizenship.

Just as had been the case with property, a tendency emerged here to convert conditions into essences and means into ends. In the 1960s and 1970s, social rights came to be considered by many as the core of citizenship. The equality between citizens to them was, at its core, social equality. Political equality then became merely one aspect of a more general equality that ought to obtain between citizens in a democratic society. It is illustrative that the talk was about a democratic "society" and that the term "republic," which refers only to the public-political sphere, was seldom heard.

TO WORK OR NOT TO WORK, IS THAT THE QUESTION?

During the 1980s, however, these debates changed direction. By then, unemployment was high, jobs had became scarce, and the continuation of welfare state arrangements was seen as problematic. Thatcherite policies of reform and retrenchment, as well as sharp new right thinking, became influential and dominated the political agenda. The implementation of the social rights entailed in citizenship was increasingly criticized. Mead (1986) argued that the actual assignment of these rights also had to be an exercise in citizenship, and that the American practice, which in his view was lax and in which the state failed to impose its authority, did not meet this requirement. If the realization of social rights is a realization of citizenship, he argued, then the duties of citizens would have to be dealt with in combination with the rights of citizens.

This theme of social duties became widely discussed in Western welfare states. In The Netherlands, two shifts occurred in this discussion. The first concerned the foundation of duties, and the second involved making the relationship between rights and duties more dynamic. In Mead's view, the social rights and duties were conceived of as a part of citizenship. In The Netherlands, people reasoned in terms of contract: Quid pro quo, rights "naturally" entail duties. If you fail to fulfill your duties, you may not enjoy your rights. And because social rights are part of citizenship, you may, by failing to fulfill the corresponding duties, through your own fault damage your citizenship, which may (partly and temporarily) be withheld or taken away from you. In this way, citizenship was made to depend on a "contract" (the quotation marks signify the lack of voluntariness and of alternatives). This does not fit Mead's line of thought. In his view, citizenship takes central place, and duties and rights are derived from it—a perspective that many of his followers inverted. The second shift in the Dutch debate by which it diverged from Mead involved moving away from his strong emphasis on duties. Dutch discussions emphasized the dynamic and activating character of mutual relations—not just between rights and duties, but also between the citizen/employee/person drawing benefits and the state/employer/department providing benefits (Langman 1992).

The general acceptance of Marshall's incorporation of socioeconomic rights in the notion of citizenship, in combination with the problematic development of employment and social security, has led to employment taking up a central position in discussions on citizenship. Whereas Hannah Arendt (1959) still believed that citizenship could be realized only for people who were free from the concerns and burdens of labor, in many contemporary discussions, having a job is presented as *the* key to citizenship. Willingness to work becomes the paramount duty of the citizen. Work becomes the most important learning route for citizens. Putting more people to work is thought of as a way to solve various problems simultaneously, or at least to reduce them to bearable proportions: Social security would remain affordable (more premiums, fewer allowances); the national economy would flourish and remain competitive; law enforcement would improve (employees are more law-abiding and more easily traced); and social integration would be stimulated (people who work participate more than those who do not).

Even if the parenthetic assumptions are correct, one might well object to making employment such a central issue of citizenship. The civic position of the unemployed is thereby further marginalized. Unpaid activities are undervalued. Those working part-time become part-citizens. All of the intractable problems involved in distinguishing between the deserving and the undeserving poor are brought back onto the political agenda—among them the invasion of privacy and the unproductive game of blaming the victim or blaming the state (Whose "fault" is it, when someone does not have a job?). A civic duty to work is imposed on people without an income from property—a duty that wealthy citizens do not bear. This conflicts with political equality, which should hold irrespective of private wealth or poverty.

From the point of view of citizenship, the most important objection to giving paid work such a central position is that political say and freedom are made dependent on good conduct elsewhere, outside the public-political sphere. Just as happened in earlier epochs with property and with social rights, there is a fatal confusion here between means and goals (or between conditions and essence), which in fact undermines or denies the very idea of citizenship. The point of citizenship is that it provides a public sanctuary from which dependencies that exist elsewhere, including those of (the obligation to) work, can be modified. The criterion is that those dependencies should not be such that their continued existence actually blocks access to the public sanctuary where citizenship is exercised. The accessibility of this sanctuary should depend as little as possible on conduct and positions outside that sanctuary. All discussions on citizenship that make work the central issue clash with this nucleus of citizenship.

SOCIAL RIGHTS ARE NOT CITIZEN RIGHTS

The foregoing considerations lead to an impasse. Marshall (1950), and at a later stage, Dahrendorf (1988:148–149), with good reason emphasized socioeconomic security for all as a basis of citizenship for all. However, making socioeconomic rights so absolute eventually undermined the citizenship they were devised to protect. Mead's emphasis on the implementation of welfare state arrangements as exemplary and standardizing exercises in citizenship was a necessary corrective. If social security and social assistance are to serve citizenship, their actual procurement should be considered also with regard to its effects on the reproduction of citizenship. However, Mead's inclination to make the duties absolute also undermines citizenship. What position should we take, then? Are social rights citizen rights? There seem to be good reasons for both affirming and denying this proposition. What orientation does neorepublicanism provide here? Can it help us out of the impasse?

The confusion in thinking about work, income, and citizenship can, I think, be avoided by insisting on a limited conception of citizenship as political equality. In this neorepublican view, social and economic rights and duties are not regarded as civic rights and duties. Although they are unmistakably important to citizenship, that is no reason to turn them into elements of citizenship.

On closer examination, Marshall's incorporation of social rights in citizenship does not seem advisable. Confusion was created, and later the opposite of what he intended to achieve was realized: being out of work again became an obstacle for access to citizenship. Conflicts about the organization of social security and assistance are also fought out now by means of conflicts about empirical and normative definitions of citizenship. In this way, the core and source of citizenship is under threat of removal from the public-political sphere to that of work.

This point of view does not imply that social security is not (or should not be) a matter of rights and duties. However, the rights and duties involved in (the willingness to) work are not identical with the rights and duties of citizens. Sanctions in the area of work may have the side effect of harming or curtailing the rights of citizenship. Such a side effect can be compared to that of being imprisoned because of unpaid debts, for instance. This surely restricts the citizen's freedom. Yet, the sanction is not imposed as a reaction to the violation of a citizen's duty in the strict sense. (In a broad sense, sanctioning can be regarded as a reaction to a person's failure to abide by the law. However, everyone on a particular territory—not just the citizens—has a duty to comply with the law of that territory.) Having rights in the area of work and income is of crucial importance to citizenship, but this does not make them into citizen rights. Having rights in the sphere of family and schooling is also of crucial importance to citizenship; but again, this does not make them into citizen rights. These are rights that aim to secure the conditions for access to citizenship, but they are not rights by which citizenship can allow itself to be defined. Citizenship marks a sanctuary, a place of freedom, whereas these rights concern release from unfreedom, access to that sanctuary. The same holds, mutatis mutandis, for the duties connected with these rights.

For most people, work and social security are important access routes to citizenship, just as family and school are. Furthermore, these access routes should, in principle, be open to all and should therefore be guaranteed by the state insofar as is possible. When persons cannot on their own meet the conditions of citizenship, such as having sufficient means of existence, the state or another institution should assist them. In doing this, the state may surely require from the persons involved that they contribute whatever they can. After all, it was precisely the fact that they "could not," or more precisely, "could not independently" meet the requirements of citizenship that justified the state's provision of security and assistance. Means testing for welfare recipients, or an obligation to seriously apply for jobs or to retrain in the case of unemployment, are not incompatible with neorepublican citizenship. However, the content of citizenship should not be determined by these. The power to define citizenship should not be located in procedures that help people fulfill the requirements for citizenship. Although to most people work and social security, like school and family, provide the most important access routes to citizenship, these should not be made absolute. Other ways of access may be less commonly used and nonetheless legitimate.

Consequently, neorepublican citizenship implies neither a general duty to work nor a right to a basic income. It does, however, imply the right to assistance for those who cannot independently and fully comply with the conditions of access to citizenship. Within the frame of this assistance, a duty to work and a right to income may hold in some circumstances, when one's own means of existence are insufficient.

The demarcation between jobholding and citizenship advocated here does not forbid all consideration of issues of employment and social security from the point of view of citizenship. On the contrary, in the neorepublican view, such considerations are legitimate and desirable. Yet, the evaluation of arrangements for work and social security as to their implications for citizenship is only compulsory on the question of their effectiveness in avoiding slavery—that is, in modifying dependencies in such a way that their characteristics of slavery are removed. Social security, schooling, a substitute income, and having work are means to achieve this goal, but their efficacy varies according to circumstances. Work can increase independence, but the thought that it does so by definition is incorrect. In Holland, we have known the *Arbeitseinsatz* (forced labor assignment during World War II), and we have contemporary forms of slavery in the guise of greenhouse agriculture and prostitution. Apart from cases of slavery, no compelling conclusions with regard to citizenship may be drawn from an evaluation of arrangements for work and social security. Work may activate, stimulate political and social participation, and create "normality" and community feeling. Work for and by everyone may be promoted in view of these consequences; but it may not be compellingly imposed on everyone, or on all healthy adults, as a civic duty.

Neorepublican citizenship requires actual political equality and political participation as well as a guarantee of access to equality and participation. This guarantee may not be effectuated by imposing social equality and a social duty to work, which would be merely to make one route by which the guarantee can be effectuated into the ultimate goal.

THIRD AGE CITIZENS

It is remarkable and sad, in my view, that governments in liberal democracies should try to improve the vitality of citizenship by focusing on work, precisely in a period when paid and regular jobs are becoming scarce. How can citizenship for all be realized through means that are not accessible for all? It is the more remarkable, and sadder, that governments do so in a time when their societies allow a great number of people to live without work or with part-time work. Think of the elderly, the disabled, and the unemployed. Many of these are in what Peter Laslett (1989) has called "the third age." The first and fourth ages are periods of dependency, of being born and growing up and of withering away and dying. The second age is the period of responsibility and of working for a living, and saving. In the third age are those who are free to do what they always wanted to do. Those include not only the elderly with pensions but also young artists and independent younger people who refuse to engage in the rat race but nevertheless generate an income.

At present (for how long, no one knows), many liberal democracies are rich enough to make this kind of living possible for many. Whether they can decide to do so and can find ways to divide their riches in such a way as to actualize those possibilities for many is another question. Emphasizing the duty to work will not help to heal social divisions but will rather increase the gap between those who can and those who cannot get a job and generate income. Would it not be better to concentrate on the question of real citizenship for the increasing number of persons who find themselves—willingly or not—in the third age? In terms of the currently prevailing social institutions and conventions, they are superfluous people. They vacation off season, when resorts are empty. If they are asked to serve, it is usually in intermediate social organizations and in subordinate or ornamental roles, and seldom on boards that give them positions of real power and influence. Social institutions that regulate access to power and prestige are increasingly linked to work and thus to those in the second age, precisely at a time when the ranks of those in the third age are swelling. It is a legitimate policy to aim at a certain balance between the numbers of those in the second and third ages respectively. But this should not be done by linking social institutions more tightly to work and by leaving those who are in the third age in an institutional desert that they can fill only with their private initiatives. That is a recipe for creating a new brand of second-class citizens. Citizenship for all will not be realized along this route.

TEN

□   □   □

Moral Unity or a Steady Diet
of Conflicts?

In the previous chapters, I argued that the actual organization of plurality in a context of public institutions is constitutive of citizenship. I criticized the tendency of many studies to reduce citizenship to its conditions, to focus on its social conditions and on access to it, instead of on its actual exercise. However, this is not to say that citizens can exist in a sociomoral vacuum. Conditions do matter. The point is to understand where and how, as well as the nature of those conditions. Vital citizenship is not reproduced by its own activities alone but needs also to be fed from sources that generate new recruits.

Social and moral conditions matter in two ways for citizenship. First, one may ask whether they make access to citizenship reasonably possible for all. Second, one may ask whether they make for participation by a sufficient number of people in a responsible way. Up to now, I have repeatedly emphasized the importance of the first question; in this chapter, I address the second. In Part 2 of this book, entitled "What Citizens Do," we explored the meaning of citizenship for those who exercise it. But how many are they? Is the number of people who take citizenship seriously sufficient to make it a vital component in the (re)constitution of the republic? And among those who do use their citizen rights, are there enough people who do so in a responsible way, and not entirely selfishly? These questions concern the vitality of citizenship.

The vitality of citizenship is difficult to observe and measure directly. If citizenship is a reserve circuit to be activated in unstructured situations of emergency, when the normal institutions of the republic cannot function as usual, looking at behavior in quiet times does not tell you much. Neo-republicanism does not require that all participate every day, but obviously it cannot work if only a very few ever bother to act as citizens. Nor can it work when those who participate without exception act unmorally and/or selfishly. Because the vitality of citizenship is difficult to observe, it is easy to worry about. This is precisely what many people, particularly rulers and intellectuals, do.

Vitality depends on social and moral conditions that foster it. When vitality is perceived as being dangerously low, therefore, responsible people will be tempted to create or stimulate those conditions. Such an effort, I shall argue, must usually come to naught. It is possible and advisable to protect and foster these sources of citizenship; but when they are lacking, it is not usually possible to bring them about in order to boost citizenship. The manipulative nature of such efforts is incompatible with the spontaneous and voluntary character of most of the social and moral sources that make for vital citizenship.

That there are such sources everyone agrees. Opinions differ, however, as to what those sources are. As they do with regard to the question whether these sources can be brought about or strengthened by education, political action, persuasion, or administrative arrangements. This chapter focuses on the calls for moral regeneration and for restoration of moral community that have recently arisen in a number of countries (Etzioni 1995 and 1996). It focuses, in particular, on two manifestations of this movement, namely appeals by Dutch politicians for more civic responsibility and arguments by intellectuals for a reevaluation of nationalism. It will contrast the moral unity that is the goal of these appeals with the resilience that inheres in the diversity of civil society—that lives, in Hirschman's words (1995:243), on "a steady diet of conflicts," on the actual organization of plurality by citizens.

In Chapter 4, I argued that consensus is neither a necessary nor a sufficient condition for citizens' living peacefully together. This conclusion applies also to moral unity. Why, then, bother to pay attention to those who call for moral unity? Because from the thesis that moral unity is neither sufficient nor indispensable, it by no means follows that it has no value whatsoever for vital citizenship. Of course morality makes a difference. In the following, anyway, I shall assume that morality matters to citizenship. I shall, for the sake of argument, assume that it is desirable both that people are moral and that there be a certain moral harmony or unity between them. What will be questioned are the efforts to reinstate the desired morality by calling for moral unity. Such moralizing is both counterproductive and inappropriate in a republic of citizens who freely organize their differences. Consensus or moral unity may be the outcome of their activities, but it is not a requirement that should be met before citizens begin to act.

POLITICIANS MORALIZING ABOUT CIVIC RESPONSIBILITY

In The Netherlands, during the first half of the 1990s, several leading politicians voiced their concern about the civic responsibility of the Dutch. They linked various social problems, such as criminality and bad health, with the decline of moral standards that they claimed to observe in society. The politicians' concern was concentrated on two issues: the disintegration of Dutch society and the overburdening of systems of democracy and law.

They observed that not much was left of the ordered, well-organized society of some time ago. Most people appreciate the increased freedom that came with individualism. The politicians pointed out that there is a shadow side to this development. Individualization, emancipation, and differentiation may result in social disintegration. When disintegration occurs, people think only of themselves, and feel no responsibility for the community; they do not exercise social control by holding each other accountable; for their needs, they call upon the state; they try to buy out of their duty to care for their kin and their neighbors by way of insurance premiums; or they even avoid paying dues and taxes. In short, citizens are said to be selfish and no longer to believe in the basic standards and values of the society. The politicians insisted that this trend toward disintegration has disastrous consequences.

First, disintegration was claimed to be harmful to the good life of the citizens themselves. Prime Minister Ruud Lubbers stated that a growing number of people had become recipients of massive and anonymous social care. People who depended on this care would be placed outside the community or feel left out of it. They would become isolates, mere clients of the systems of the welfare state. A political system that allowed this to happen would have forsaken its important task of integrating citizens into the national community in such a way that they can flourish in society and can participate in its social processes.

Minister of Justice Ernst Hirsch Ballin was especially concerned about another result of the trend toward disintegration: It would undermine the very basis of the constitutional state. A *Rechtsstaat*, a regime under the rule of law, requires not only that the state guarantee the legal rights of the citizens but also that the latter feel actively responsible for maintaining them. Social disintegration jeopardizes citizens' attitude of responsibility toward the community, without which the realization of formal rights will remain defective.

A third aspect of the trend toward disintegration was emphasized by Eelco Brinkman—at the time, leader of the Christian Democratic party in parliament. He worried about the effect of disintegration on public support for the welfare state. As citizens increasingly rely upon government care instead of on communal responsibilities, it becomes difficult to keep up the necessary level of provisions for those who really need them.

These three concerns are of course closely related. They express the view that citizens lack community-mindedness and a feeling of responsibility, without which the policies of the welfare state cannot work. Therefore, the speechmakers concluded, a contribution to the solution of the problems of the welfare state will, to a large extent, have to come from the community itself. This is where politicians join each other in an appeal for civic responsibility. To them, this means active citizenship, which is expressed not only in loyalty to the law and political participation in a narrow sense but also in the acceptance of responsibility for oneself and others, in one's contributions to social life. Civic responsibility is conceived of not only as pertaining to the sphere of the state but also as a leading principle outside the public-political realm.

The second issue politicians were concerned about was the overburdening of democracy and the legal system. A dangerous pincer movement was said to be taking place: On the one hand, citizens increasingly were turning to politicians and the courts to promote their interests and rights, and on the other, they increasingly failed to obey laws and regulations. They used the legal and democratic systems as it suited them, as consumers, without accepting responsibility for the continuing functioning of those systems. The latter were becoming overused and overburdened. The politicians admitted that the government itself was also to blame. Not only had it made too many laws and regulations but it also had contributed to the "pollution of standards" by placing insufficient emphasis on the moral content of legal rules, by making obscure regulations, by failing to enforce the law, and often by not abiding by its own rules. However, the citizens were also criticized. They were said to show calculating behavior and to accept moral standards, if they knew them at all, in the abstract but not to adhere to them in practice. It was time for a new public morality: In line with the requirement that the government learn a new way of governing, the citizen was expected to develop a new lifestyle in which civic responsibility should have a central position. In this context, "civic responsibility" would mean abiding by the laws and rules and holding others accountable for doing the same.

The emphasis on responsibilities and duties, the politicians insisted, involved more than a smart attempt to curtail the cost of government provisions or to guarantee compliance with the law. Making individual citizens accountable for their own deeds and omissions, they argued, would be a sign of respect for who and what citizens are, an indication that they truly belong to the community as full members. Experiencing and fulfilling duties would give the community the chance to care for the people who really do need care, and it would give the citizen the chance to grow from an object of care to a subject of integration and freedom.

These interventions of the politicians aroused mixed feelings in the population at large and in the news media in particular. Undeniably, they were addressing important matters; but something was wrong with what the politicians were saying. Or was it the way in which, or the position from which, they said it? In order to clarify these misgivings, I shall analyze the sayings of the politicians by considering them as speech acts: What did the politicians *do* by giving these speeches? Three things, it seems to me:

1. They drew inspiration from the past.
2. They misapprehended contemporary plurality.
3. They spoke to the responsible citizens, who were present, about the calculating citizens, who were absent.

These three aspects of the speech acts of politicians are analyzed below.

THE PAST AS COMPASS:
FILTH, DANGER, AND PURIFICATION RITUALS

Drawing inspiration from the past is a well-known strategy for political renewal. Revolutions and revolutionaries model themselves on the past. To the Romans, an appeal to authority (*auctoritas*) meant a return to the source, to the act of foundation of Rome. When we get stuck, in quarrels or otherwise, we also return to the acts, to the binding decisions and agreements that constituted our relationship. Protestants return to the Acts of the Apostles, as they were laid down in the Bible. By returning to the source, future deterioration and corruption may be fought.

This is done by way of rituals of confirmation and purification. Confirmation rituals take us back to the original source, which regenerates us and gives our common actions direction and power. Before we are able and allowed to get to the pure source, we must cleanse ourselves and the community from impure elements. Without purification, there is no regeneration. Purification rituals vary from washing off graffiti to executing traitors.

Dirt is matter that is out of place. It disturbs the (correct) order. Dirt that has to be washed off stands for danger—the danger of disintegration and lack of direction of the community. "Foreign commentators in one voice criticize the pollution and danger in the streets of the large Dutch cities," wrote the minister of justice (Hirsch Ballin 1992). Complaints about morally degenerate behavior, about filth on the neighbor's balcony, about dog shit in the street, and about carelessness, mean more than they seem to at first. They signify danger: Dirt is evidence of the activities of a pol-luter, a breaker of order who is dangerous. Dirt also bears the risk of in-fection. Purification and the cutting out of tumors may be needed to pre-vent illnesses from spreading. And if such an isolation of dangerous dirt is not possible, then an equally dangerous and potentially polluting med-icine may prove necessary as an antidote.

This vocabulary of dirt, danger, illness, and regeneration can be recog-nized in contemporary arguments about civic responsibility. A compari-son with older strategies and vocabularies of political renewal makes one realize the extent to which current experiences of pollution and danger may be determined by the notions of order that people currently hold. Where one person sees plurality, the other sees rubbish. Where one per-son sees variety, another sees disorder. Where the one sees monsters (un-acceptable combinations such as centaurs), the other sees fascinating nov-elties. Someone who fears that order will collapse is bound to see many dangers. If dirt is a sign of danger, then such a person will have a lot of cleansing to do.

In view of these considerations, frequent manifestations of concern about a lack of civic responsibility first and foremost indicate a fear that order will collapse. That is, someone's fear and someone's conception of order. The question of whether an acceptable order in political or social interaction is actually in danger cannot be decided simply by referring to a particular politician's idea of order. This is so because politics is pre-cisely about conflicting conceptions of order and ways of dealing with them. Conflicting conceptions of order, which are mutually felt to be threatening, are bound to generate experiences of deterioration and pol-lution. Politics, therefore, is inherently dirtier than many other human ac-tivities and relations.

The past cannot, strictly speaking, be brought back, but it is precisely this impossibility that enables politicians to mobilize and manipulate it for the purpose of contemporary repairs. "Pillarization" (the division of society into nonoverlapping segments) in The Netherlands, for instance, is a thing of the past. It may, however, serve as an example of what is pos-sible—of what we Dutch once were able to do and should therefore be able to do again. It may serve as a model of and a model for a workable political community. Politicians want citizens to conform to such models.

However, this wish poses a problem. In the models, the source of civic responsibility traditionally has been located outside the public-political sphere—in a strict religion (De Tocqueville); in the rhythm of working in industry (Durkheim); in discipline in schools and other institutions (Fou-cault); or in the family. Politicians look for sources of civic responsibility outside the public-political sphere. But where should they look? In con-temporary society, there is little unity of culture and ways of life. We find religious people and nonbelievers; people who are subjected to the discipline of a "regular" job and those who do irregular work or have no job; ambitious students and dropouts; families and other forms of cohabitation. While becoming more varied, religion, work, school and family have also become less all-embracing.

We live in a plural society where civic responsibility primarily arises *in* the interaction between pluralities in the public-political sphere. Politicians do have a task here, but they cannot adequately fulfill it by moralizing and by making appeals to other spheres. The public-social and private spheres to a large extent no longer work the way the politicians assume in their interventions. They are rightly worried about disintegration and selfishness in the democratic welfare state; but in their attempts to save democracy, they deny the very plurality that democracy exists to advance and organize.

The theme of democracy being ruined by its own freedom is an old one. Democracy implies the freedom of the individual to live the way he sees fit, to do whatever he wants to do, within the limits of the law. This freedom may lead to calculating egoism and narcissism, or to a loss of self-control and civility. According to Plato, he who restlessly tries to satisfy his momentary desires is not free. He is addicted, a slave to his own desires. He who is ruled by his own desires is not a citizen. A democracy that has gone too far, that is mainly populated by such addicts, was traditionally regarded as susceptible to tyranny. People follow the demagogue who promises them instant satisfaction of their desires. (The narcissist sees himself in the mirror the demagogue represents. He identifies with the leader and feels perfectly represented, for as long as the identification lasts.) In classical republicanism, civic virtue was supposed to act as a barrier against such derailments.

It is difficult to soberly assess such dangers and to deal with them in a reasonable way. Consider the trouble that members of parliaments have in determining their position with regard to their colleagues on the extreme right. They have a hard time trying to find a balance between ignoring and fighting them. Those who easily see dangers (who want to recognize and fight them "in time") in their eagerness to defend democracy actually jeopardize plurality, and with it, democracy itself. Democracy can be ruined by paranoia, suspicion, and the inability to adequately organize and tolerate inconvenient plurality. The refrain of complaints about insufficient civic responsibility can be found in Plato's work, where he quotes Socrates as having said: "For I am told that Pericles made the Athenians idle and cowardly and talkative and covetous, because he was the first to establish pay for service among them" (*Gorgias* 515).

Thus, civic responsibility is not an innocent topic but an explosive one. Those who seek to heal and save the "sick society" or the unbridled democracy by way of a reorientation toward the community that is said to have existed in former times run the risk of do-gooders in the public sphere. In the words of contemporary thinker Eli Sagan, whose analysis of Athenian democracy offers an original combination of political and psychoanalytic insight: "The total paranoid control promised by all schemes of social engineering and by totalitarian societies are attempts to heal the terrible wounds caused by the destruction of kinship forms of social solidarity. They create, in phantasy or in reality, a solidarity more inflexible, more controlling, more overwhelming than any kinship system ever provided" (Sagan 1991:146).

Yet we do need a source of inspiration, orientation, and identity. This we have to find and give shape to, however, *in* the present context. An appeal to a source does not work when it implies a denial of current social reality. In such a denial, the source becomes the opposite of what is wrong now. The ideal then becomes: contemporary society minus its shortcomings. Such an ideal is fed by resentment about how society now works and by a failure to accept the present (with its plurality, immigrants, and uninterested people). Resentment and nostalgia are not good guidelines. The present is not an anomaly that can or should be erased as quickly as possible.

The speech-making politicians regard contemporary society as an objectionable fact, a source of problems they have to concoct a solution for. They do not want reality as it is but as it would surface in its improved form from their interventions. They seem to be wondering: Why do citizens not participate in what is good for them? Why are they so stubborn or indifferent? If only they showed civic responsibility, our tasks would be less unmanageable. In the old days, people used to participate. In the old days, yes. . . . When a social, cultural, and normative orientation toward the past is combined with a pragmatic-technological orientation toward the future, we have a conservatism that at first may look reasonable but that as we know from bitter experience, is in fact a volatile mixture.

MULTIPLE CALCULATIONS
WITHOUT ONE ULTIMATE STANDARD

An orientation toward the past has consequences for the observation of contemporary plurality, which is viewed in terms of how it used to be. We shall see that this orientation leads to a misperception and misjudgment of contemporary society and its possibilities. Contemporary society is indeed offensive as well as exciting, and it does show disintegrative tendencies. Old associations are falling apart or losing influence. One can no longer trust them or implicitly rely on the behavior of their members.

New associations, such as temporary employment agencies, futures markets, old people's organizations, organized crime, and various protest-oriented social movements, come and go before they have found an acceptable and recognizable place within established decisionmaking structures and data collections. The categories by means of which we classify reality and make it manageable, such as those of the Central Bureau of Statistics, or political parties, are broken through, time and again. They provide an insufficient grip on what we want to grasp. The dynamic and multiform social reality—or should we say realities?—is not readily represented either in parliament or other representative bodies, or in the classifying work of economists, sociologists, and other scientists.

Is there a guaranteeing story, a founding principle that keeps this recondite plurality manageable and acceptable? People used to find such reassurance in the "hidden hand" (Adam Smith); in the dialectic of history (Hegel, Marx); in combating prejudice (the Enlightenment); in discussions, in hearing both sides, and in technological pragmatism. Nowadays, however, the belief that such a founding principle exists has disappeared. Each attempt to construct an authoritative metastory is suspect. Each attempt to tell such a story is distrusted as concealed tyranny.

The task and place of politics are no longer guaranteed in a metastory, either. Politics—that is, we participants in plural society—must itself maintain and renew its legitimacy. The place and task of politics are not guaranteed by the standards of "the" Dutch culture. That culture is not unitary but plural. Therefore an appeal for civic responsibility cannot refer to a common cultural standard the existence of which is taken for granted.

Misled by an imaginary stability in the past, the politicians construct a false opposition between the calculating and the responsible citizen. They misperceive the indispensable role of calculation in the organization of plurality, or for that matter, in any modern form of social order. Even some slaves had to calculate in order to do their work. So much more the citizen. The appeal to the citizens to adhere to standards and not to take a calculating attitude is simply inappropriate. The citizen who complies with this by not calculating will often disturb the organization of plurality. After all, calculation is indispensable in the organization of changing plurality and in the formation of a judgment about what constitutes a sensible application of standards. We count on each other's calculation—without it, the organization of contemporary plurality is inconceivable.

Calculation and adherence to moral or legal standards are not opposites. Without standards, there is no calculation. Calculation presupposes the attribution of value to the elements that are part of the calculation, as well as rules concerning the combination of these elements. In the evaluation of the usefulness and appropriateness of calculations in a certain situation, standards and calculation play a role. Moreover, calculation is in order with regard to standards and their appropriateness. Think, for instance, of the judicial tenets of force majeure and of self-defense, which require people to make judgments based on quantitative estimates of risks and dangers. In order to establish proportionality between a threat and one's reactions to it, one must calculate proportions. Calculation is allowed and is part of the normal behavior of citizens.

The law both promotes and restricts calculation. Think, for instance, of the doctrine of the lawful act of government, which states that certain government actions are not unlawful as long as the government pays for the (calculated) damage resulting from its actions. Calculation is thus used to organize accountability. Calculation is thinking in terms of consequences, taking into account that . . . . Consultants, lawyers, and officials of an unemployment agency or a business firm assist their citizens/clients by making calculations in their behalf. Calculation is an indispensable element in the normative organization of social interaction.

PARADOXICAL COMMUNICATION AND THE ETHICS OF THE "BLANK CHECK"

Who exactly are the people to whom appeals for civic responsibility are being addressed? The active citizens, or those who are uninterested? Are companies, consultants, children, and stay-at-homes included? Are people who live inside the country without having citizen status included? The lack of interest of citizens is criticized in speeches that in fact are addressed to those who were interested enough to come and listen. The politicians' criticism, however, is directed at those who don't hear their statements, the outsiders who did not come to listen. Thus, what the speakers are doing in essence is to rally the insiders against the uninterested outsiders. Below, more will be said about uninterested citizens. Here, we consider first the people for whom the appeals are primarily meant, the good citizens who have come to listen. An appeal directed at them also poses problems—namely, paradoxical communication, and the colonization of their life-world.

Paradoxical communication arises when the act of communication denies the content of the message that is communicated (Elster 1983). "Be spontaneous"—the act of commanding conflicts with the content of the message. Such communication leaves its hearers feeling perplexed, sensing that they are in a double bind. Imposing civic responsibility on free citizens, or talking them into it, is experienced as inappropriate by many. "I'll be the judge of that" is an oft-heard reaction to appeals for civic responsibility.

One could argue that such a reaction is uncalled for, because these are attempts of citizens to convince their cocitizens. It is not that simple, however. These attempts to convince cocitizens, after all, are being made by people who as officeholders have a compulsory relationship of authority to those they address. To many, a cabinet minister is not simply a cocitizen when he is giving a speech. Yet, accusations of a lack of civic responsibility also have their problems in a debate between free and equal citizens. By making such accusations, the speaker implicitly questions the citizenship, the free and equal status, of the person addressed. Whichever way one looks at it, appeals for civic responsibility retain a paradoxical aspect in almost all situations. Citizenship is the basis on which convictions and appeals between citizens may develop. Rarely can this basis itself be protected against erosion by way of appeals.

"Colonization of the life-world" is a phrase used by Jürgen Habermas (1981:476). Systems of health care, finance, higher education, and the like require system-conforming behavior from ordinary people in order to be reasonably controllable and to render their system-products. If such behavior is to be relied on, it should be rooted in the life-world of the people involved. Yet, this world often generates standards and behavior, traditional or not, that do not fit the requirements of modern system-management. Traditional or life-world ethics thus conflicts with modern system-ethics. Such a conflict very clearly emerges in environmental issues. For the purpose of preserving the environment, of system-preservation, we are invited by experts on the system to believe their (often inadequately tested) elaborations and to act accordingly (Wildavsky 1995). We are required to do what is necessary for the preservation of systems on which we are dependent for our survival. Essentially, we are being asked to adopt an "empty" ethics, to provide a blank check; in concrete terms, possibly to act against our deepest convictions. The linking of traditionally substantive values to a formal willingness to conform to system requirements is problematic. It leads to ambiguity in the appeals for civic responsibility. Which kind of civic responsibility is called for? The one that is traditional in content or the one that supports system-steering?

THE UNINTERESTED CITIZEN

We now turn to the uninterested citizen, the black sheep in the politicians' speeches. Why, actually, would it be wrong for a citizen to be uninterested? After all, in post–World War II theorizing on democracy, apathy often was regarded as positive. Enthusiastic participation by many, it was said, would easily lead to polarization, ideologization, and intolerance. It would create totalitarian democracy and might result in civil war. Political elites that were pragmatic and willing to compromise, and relatively inactive and obedient masses, were regarded as conditions for a stable democracy. Today, this theory offers us no solutions, because the new uninterested citizens, unlike their counterparts in the 1950s, do not spontaneously behave "properly," that is, in line with the good citizens. They "misbehave." Whereas apathy used to be regarded as good for democracy, lack of interest now is seen as undermining it.

In their speeches, Dutch politicians indicate four major problems, the solution to which, in their view, would be thwarted by citizens' lack of interest:

1. Maintaining the law and keeping society governable;
2. Mutual care and the preservation of national solidarity in the welfare state;
3. Political participation and the viability of democracy;
4. Participation in employment and the viability of the social market economy.

By fighting lack of interest and by promoting civic responsibility, the politicians hope to contribute to the solution of these problems. Can this be done, and is it permissible? Let us first examine whether it can be done.

As we saw earlier, in contemporary society, there is no longer one source, such as Christian upbringing, from which a unified and active citizenry might come forth. The ways of learning that lead to the qualities required under the four points above are nowadays relatively unconnected. Someone who becomes more helpful does not thereby become more law-abiding or politically more active. Extensive political participation leaves too little time for the work and the quick decisionmaking required by the market. The spheres mentioned above—of law, care, politics, and employment—have developed their own independence and logic in spite of their mutual intertwining. An appeal for civic responsibility cannot bring unity here.

If these problems cannot be handled by a single solution, could we not take a more modest approach by promoting civic responsibility per area or sector? We might focus on the interest that the uninterested citizens have in receiving and maintaining community provisions. This interest would have to be made visible: Those who are already aware of it but who do not want to pay the price in the form of a contribution would have to be made to see negative effects on their income or freedom. They would have to see that their behavior was no longer paying off. The administration of justice, provision of care, mediation of employment, and administration of social security thus would become disciplinary institutions. People have to be shown and told how things are, and those who do not want to listen should be made to feel.

In practice, however, very little good comes of such an approach. The policymaking bodies remain anonymous to indifferent people, and individual executive civil servants usually have little real disciplining power. They are often threatened by clients, and they cannot do much, having no leeway for improvisation. Disciplining power works only in situations that occur within total institutions—that is, institutions that encompass many aspects of life. Even prisons and schools no longer work that way today.

Next, we come to the question of whether it is permissible to fight a lack of interest as the opposite of civic responsibility. With regard to the public-political sphere, various positions can be distinguished: slave (will-less follower), citizen (partly giving shape), enemy (undermining), contractor-consumer (taking advantage). From a neorepublican perspective, the latter cannot be rejected and combated: Citizens have a right to be uninterested. (Specific obligations in specific situations—such as serving on a jury—may take priority over this right.) No more obligations may be imposed on citizens who lack interest than on others. The conditions set for citizens, uninterested or otherwise, are the same.

Is lack of interest on the part of citizens actually bad? Assuming that it were allowed and could be effective, would it make sense to fight such lack of interest? The answer is complex: Lack of interest, ignoring each other, is often a successful way of dealing with plurality. Moreover, allowing for a lack of interest is essential for a free society's functioning (Zinoviev 1981; Elster 1983; Hirschman 1970). People who simply turn away, who take the option of exit, provide important signals on the road of peaceful change in a free society. Not only do companies learn from customers who walk away from their products, but political parties, systems of care, and systems of law may learn from uninterest as well. A mixture of loyal and uninterested citizens works best. Those who take the exit-option give a tangible signal, which starts a process of change that is supported by the loyal citizens. Having only loyal citizens results in blindness; having only uninterested citizens, in powerlessness.

The acknowledgment of people's freedom not to be interested—to be neither for nor against but indifferent or simply interested in matters other than citizenship—breaks through the smothering logic of "those who are not for us are against us." Internal contradiction (something is either *a* or *b*) works differently from external contradiction (something is either *a* or non-*a*; but being non-*a* does not mean that it is *b*). The East European communist regimes acted so stupidly, were so stuck, and needed such immense secret services because, among other things, they were caught in the logic of internal contradiction, of friend or foe. In free republics, a similar logic surfaces regularly, but it also can be freely combated. For instance, the choice "for or against Europe [meaning the European Union]" can be refused, as can the choice "civic responsibility or lack of interest."

Equating lack of interest with lack of civic responsibility is inappropriate not only because a citizen has the right to be uninterested but also because too many essentially different positions are concealed by the phrase "lack of interest." There are free riders; and there are others who appear to be taking advantage, who are interested in the common cause but secretly refrain from contributing whenever they have the chance. Then there are the cynics, who can adopt any position yet believe in nothing. And there are those "weak of will," people of good intentions and weak flesh. There are uninterested people who are dedicated to matters other than citizenship and who therefore, in their behavior, do not show a great deal of civic responsibility. And finally, there are real opponents and underminers of the republic. These cannot be successfully fought by allowing them to hide behind an undifferentiated screen of uninterested people who are all said to lack civic responsibility.

Our purpose in this chapter is to explore how the vitality of citizenship can be enhanced. The moral appeals of politicians are not of much help except in exemplifying what not to do. Can questions about the vitality of citizenship be better tackled if we do not take the view of politicians in positions of authority, and do not address individuals (thereby reinforcing the individualism that was precisely the problem) but the culture that encompasses them? In the next section, we look at efforts by some intellectuals to strengthen a nationalism within which a sense of citizenship can flourish.

NATURALIZING NATIONALISM

The recent resurgence of nationalist political movements and conflicts has been reflected upon by intellectuals who for a long time showed no great interest in such an outdated and imaginary phenomenon as nationalism. They describe, study, explain, and condone. Quite a few have made a change of position that may be characterized as naturalizing nationalism while simultaneously historicizing (denaturalizing) liberal democracy. This change of position is analyzed more closely below.

Not long ago, for the majority of intellectuals, nationalism was something contructed, an artifact. It was considered dangerous and to be kept strictly to its subaltern place in the political order. Nowadays, for many intellectuals who write on nationalism, it is both natural and human, containing not only vicious elements but also potential for peaceful cooperation, and forming an indispensable and central principle of political order.

How has this change of vision among intellectuals come about? To their credit, it must be said that they openly admit to have changed their positions. They report a kind of conversion, a moment when they began to see what they could not or would not see earlier. "Looking back, I see that time in the crypt as a moment when I began to change, when some element of respect for the national project began to creep into my feelings, when I understood why land and grave matter and why the nations matter which protect both" (Ignatieff 1993:93–94). Formerly, the intellectuals tell us, they had, as good liberals, contempt for nationalism. "I both disliked and disbelieved the ambient rhetoric of national decline. It struck me mostly as a suppressed form of imperial nostalgia. . . . But as I have lived here longer, I have come to see that the space for a multi-cultural, multi-racial, post-national cosmopolitanism in Britain was much narrower than I had supposed. . . . In reality, the British are among the most fiercely nationalistic of all peoples" (Ignatieff 1993:168). Tony Judt (1994:45) has written of the erstwhile historicist critics of nationalism, both liberals and Marxists: "Nationalism and national identity are taken seriously but not on their own terms, and so they elude understanding." Now, in 1994, we know better: "If we wish to counter such views we have to begin by acknowledging that they contain a kernel of truth. There *are* incommensurate goals and unresolvable problems, and the unequal and conflicted division of the world into nations and peoples is not about to wither and shrivel or be overcome by goodwill or progress" (Judt 1994:51). To see or not (yet) to see, that seems to be the question. As Paul Scheffer (1995) wrote: "What those critics [of the new acceptance of nationalism] don't see is that every society needs to procure for itself some 'minima moralia', which consist in more than universal values only."

The vision of those converted intellectuals, roughly speaking, is that nationalism *is* (belongs to living together, fulfills a basic human need) and is *necessary* (for living together). The question is no longer nationalism or not, for or against. Not whether, but only how to give it form or how to modify it. It makes no sense to ignore or fight against something that is unavoidable and indispensable.

How might we understand this collective constructive move that "enlightened" intellectuals have made with regard to nationalism? And what notions of social order are implied in their new ways of seeing? We find the makings of an answer in studies by anthropologist Mary Douglas (1975) on self-evidence and "the natural."

In every society, some things and relations are taken as self-evident, inviolable, and natural. Each culture has its own notion of nature and of the natural. This usually concerns matters and relations that are so central in the prevailing social and moral orders that all doubt about them should be banished. They are stated and repeated but by no means argued for.

Their self-evident character is confirmed in the way they are presented. What is natural does not even need argument. Who would argue against nature?

The natural is constructed in such a way that it confirms and supports the social and moral order. The central elements in this order are placed beyond criticism and argument. They are self-evident and natural. Whoever doubts them is either crazy or an insufficiently knowledgeable outsider. Unnatural behavior thus disturbs the sociomoral order, and it is therefore harmful. What is unnatural should be excluded or imprisoned. Monsters are creatures that break through "natural" classifications. Examples are the centaur, which is half man and half animal, or persons who are not legal residents in the country but who nevertheless avail themselves of social help or vote in elections (as happened in Amsterdam, in 1994). The natural orders should be kept natural and pure, both the order of things (ecology) and that of people. Governments also must respect the natural givens in society. When they fail to do this, their policies will be seen as ineffective and even harmful.

From this anthropological point of view, changing conceptions of what is natural or unavoidable signal changes in social classifications and orders. Let us look in this light at changing ideas about the naturalness of nationalism. Do we find there also the three hallmarks of the natural: (1) repeated presentation of "natural" givens without argument, (2) which support the sociomoral order and (3) which justify exclusion of what does not fit because of its unnaturalness?

Unargued and repeated insistence on the unavoidability of some form of nationalism is common to the recent confessions of intellectuals noted above. Their conversion is not a matter of arguments but rather of enlightenment that comes from outside or within but that is surely beyond argument. How do intellectuals, who after all are specialists in argument, allow themselves to become convinced without argument? By bad argument, by a presentation that looks like an argument but that on closer inspection does not hold together. There are four typical ways of doing this.

The first is the juxtaposition and interchangeable use of terms like "basic human need," "identity," "something to hold onto," "belonging," "group," "tradition," and "nationalism." The suggestion is that we, the reader and the writer, all know what these terms refer to and what their connection and communality is. In their presentation, some kind of community is suggested and imagined.

A second way to avoid argument is to present pressing problems, and then, without argument, to qualify them as problems of identity. Not every pressing political problem, however, is a problem of identity. We need to investigate how, in what circumstances, conflicts become conflicts of identity. In Gordes, in Provence, my Dutch children played the game of

Risk with French children. They hardly understood each other's language. They played well together until the words exchanged between speakers of the native tongue were "heard" by "the others" as a conspiracy to outplay the foreigners. Then the play stopped, its place being taken by a shouting match between the French and the Dutch.

A third way in which argument is avoided is to insist that something more is needed to make political democracy and the laws work than the laws themselves, and then to offer feelings of nationalism as this "something." Surely the laws need more than themselves to work, as they are not self-executing. But what this "more" involves needs argument and has been widely contested. Candidates have been the division of labor (Durkheim), disciplinary practices (Foucault), the spirit of the laws (Montesquieu), the leadership of a lawgiver (Rousseau), and, yes, nationalism. Here also, study and argument are needed to determine what principles of order, anchored in feeling and behavior, obtain and can be harnessed, and in what circumstances.

A fourth way to avoid argument and to naturalize nationalism is by essentializing situated speech. Talk about a national cabinet or the nation itself being in peril during wartime is perfectly understandable in its context. But from this it does not follow that we may study nationalism as an attitude, feeling, or essence (as a ghost in the machine, to use Ryle's term). In certain situations, the statement "you are an angel" is perfectly comprehensible, but nowadays this no longer leads to investigating the properties of angels. Why should it be otherwise with nationalism?

Naturalizing has its benefits. He who can invoke nature has reality on his side. De Schaepdrijver (1995) clearly shows this in her analysis of nationalism in Belgium:

> The essentialist vision of language groups as by definition nations, and the homogenizing assumption that multilingualism in one area by itself leads to conflicts, have for quite some time now acquired the power of self-evidence in the articulated public sphere. Thereby the "natural" evolution, of which Prime Minister Van den Brande spoke, has indeed lost its "natural" limits, and thereby the political compromise of Sint-Michiels remains operative on a pragmatic rather than on a principled basis. This merely pragmatic foundation enables separatists to paint proponents of even a merely federalized Belgium as nostalgic people, and to contrast their "emotional appeals" with the "cool reality" of the necessity of separation.

While nationalism is naturalized, liberalism is being denaturalized. How does this work? The place of liberalism in the world is basically altered by the insistence on a historically developed consensus as an indispensable element of a viable political community and as a condition for, or even a core element of, liberalism. Liberalism thereby loses its universal appeal and openness and is made into a historical product, by virtue of which it is no longer accessible to all people. The implications of such a coupling of liberalism with a particular historical culture are clearly stated in a newspaper article by the philosopher Herman Philipse (1994): "Therefore the inflow of immigrants should not become too big (also because of overpopulation in our mini-country) and we shall, with care and love, have to initiate the immigrants into the game of democracy and its concomitant public morality." Here, the implications of the naturalization of nationalism are stated without further ado: quantitative containment and the education of newcomers. Thus, nationalism ascribes certain qualities not only to us insiders but also to them, the outsiders. They are different, they lack what we have in common.

What element of the internal moral and social order is protected and expressed by this external attribution of properties to outsiders? I suggest: the internal order of useful/superfluous people and materials. In contemporary societies, much waste is being produced with great dedication: Dirt—that is, superfluous matter—and unemployment—that is, superfluous people. These accumulate in mountains of polluted earth and lines of people waiting for their turn. To increase efficiency is to do more with less and therefore to get rid of waste. In a sociomoral order centered around increasing efficiency, politics is cornered into the role of waste disposal, of ordering the superfluous.

What is usually lacking in the interventions of intellectuals concerning nationalism is content. This is understandable. Each nationalism is supposed to be unique, so what can an individual say about it? In societies that are de facto plural, each proposal to give nationalism a specific content will meet with criticism and thus fail to exemplify the consensus that it purports to have found. That something like nationalism is necessary, unavoidable, and natural is stated, but what its content is, and what should be done with dissidents, usually remains unclear. What also usually remains hidden is the constructive activity of the intellectuals themselves. Nationalism was and remains a constructed artifact. If it fulfills a human need, it does so in a culturally specific way that involves a culturally specific interpretation or construction of the particular human need. This insight is sometimes forgotten by the new nationalists. That does not mean that their constructive activities cease to exist but only that they take place in the dark, unregulated by law, politics, and empirical testing.

Liberalism recognizes the need for order but rejects any means toward order that go beyond the law, the constitution, and politics. This position was eloquently expressed by Justice Jackson of the U.S. Supreme Court (*West Virginia State Board of Education v. Barnette*, 319 U.S. 624 [1943]):

Struggles to coerce uniformity of sentiment in support of some end thought essential to their time and country have been waged by many good as well as by evil men. Nationalism is a relatively recent phenomenon but at other times and places the ends have been racial or territorial security, support of a dynasty or regime, and particular plans for saving souls. As first and moderate methods to attain unity have failed, those bent on its accomplishment must resort to an ever-increasing severity. As governmental pressure toward unity becomes greater, so strife becomes more bitter as to whose unity it shall be. Probably no deeper division of our people could proceed from any provocation than from finding it necessary to choose what doctrine and whose program public educational officials shall compel youth to unite in embracing. Ultimate futility of such attempts to compel coherence is the lesson of every such effort from the Roman drive to stamp out Christianity as a disturber of its pagan unity, the Inquisition as a means to religious and dynastic unity, the Siberian exiles as a means to Russian unity, down to the fast failing efforts of our present totalitarian enemies. Those who begin coercive elimination of dissent soon find themselves exterminating dissenters. Compulsory unification of opinion achieves only the unanimity of the graveyard. It seems trite but necessary to say that the First Amendment to our Constitution was designed to avoid these ends by avoiding these beginnings. . . . When they are so harmless to others or to the State as those we deal with here [a refusal to salute the flag], the price is not too great. But freedom to differ is not limited to things that do not matter much. That would be a mere shadow of freedom. The test of its substance is the right to differ as to things that touch the heart of the existing order.

The intellectuals who naturalize nationalism insufficiently appreciate the dangers of their striving for unity and order. They make nationalism acceptable while leaving its content underspecified. Their own brand of nationalism may look peaceful and acceptable, but they remain practically defenseless against nastier fillings of a theoretically empty shell. They conceive of national unity as an indispensable embedding for citizenship. Believing in this national unity, then, becomes a primary duty of the citizen. Without much exaggeration, one could say that while dealing with differences is the point of citizenship for neorepublicans, for the new nationalists the point of citizenship is the cultivation of a feeling of unity that overrides differences.

CIVIL SOCIETY

We have now looked at two efforts to understand and restore the sources of viable political citizenship: the politicians' appeals for civic responsibility and the intellectuals' insistence on nationalism as a natural necessity.

These efforts were found wanting, both empirically and normatively. These social engineers have views of how society works that are steered by their wish that it be orderly and governable. How should society be in order to be governable, is their leading question. What does not fit *this* imagined society is ignored or swept aside as unfitting. The political problem of organizing the plurality of disturbing differences and conflicts between people is "solved" by positing its opposite: unity. The moral unity of responsible individuals, or the historical unity of the nation. Citizens, whose task it is to deal with harsh differences among themselves, are here admitted as citizens only after they have shed their disturbing differences. Such attempts to solve problems by denial and exclusion will not work. They also result in poor social analysis and a primitive notion of social order, because the desired outcome, the unity of reliable order, is posited as the beginning: consensus. In Chapter 4, I questioned the idea underlying these approaches, that consensus is a prerequisite for social and political order.

The search for the sources of vital citizenship may thus lead to the abdication of politics and the trivialization of citizens: The task of citizens in politics is declared doable only when it has already been done—namely, in society. How are we then to conceive the relations between political citizenship and the sociomoral sources that are supposed to nurture it? The idea of civil society, with its emphasis on the dynamics of self-organization and the resilience of plurality, offers a better perspective.

A civil society is characterized by diversity and by institutions for dealing with conflicts without doing away with diversity. The institutions of civil law regulate conflicting activities of people without demanding that they share the same values. A civil society is not just any society that does not fly apart. It is neither a homogeneous community nor a market. It has elements of these but does not coincide with them. Nor can a civil society ever fully coincide with the state. There is always a distance between them that is supervised by an independent judiciary and other institutions that mediate their relations.

It is in civil society that people form their ideas and organize themselves. When ideas and concerns have grown and become robustly organized, citizens may effectively present them in the public-political sphere. The vitality of citizenship is fed by the vitality of civil society. Given this connection, it is understandable that politicians who are interested in fostering citizenship try to bring state and civil society closer together and to use state power to strengthen civil ties. In doing so, however, they often undermine what they want to foster. This is so because civil society usually remains vital only so long as the state keeps a proper distance from it. When state and civil society get too close or become identical, they both lose vitality.

In a recent study, Robert Putnam provided an explanation for this. He found that in Italy, regional government in regions with a high degree of civil association—that is, with a variety of autonomous social organizations—was stronger, in the sense of being more effective and more appreciated by citizens, than in regions where active political patronage was dominant. He also found that both types of relations between the political and social spheres were stable over time and resistant to change.

> In all societies . . . dilemmas of collective action hamper attempts to cooperate for mutual benefit, whether in politics or in economics. Third-party enforcement is an inadequate solution to this problem. Voluntary cooperation (like rotating credit associations) depends on social capital. Norms of generalized reciprocity and networks of civic engagement encourage social trust and cooperation because they reduce incentives to defect, reduce uncertainty, and provide models for future cooperation. Trust itself is an emergent property of the social system, as much as a personal attribute. Individuals are able to be trusting (and not merely gullible) because of the social norms and networks within which their actions are embedded. Stocks of social capital, such as trust, norms, and networks, tend to be self-reinforcing and cumulative. Virtuous circles result in social equilibria with high levels of cooperation, trust, reciprocity, civic engagement, and collective well-being. These traits define the civic community. Conversely, the absence of these traits in the *un*civic community is also self-reinforcing. Defection, distrust, shirking, exploitation, isolation, disorder, and stagnation intensify one another in a suffocating miasma of vicious circles. This argument suggests that there may be at least *two* broad equilibria toward which all societies that face problems of collective action . . . tend to evolve and which, once attained, tend to be self-reinforcing. (Putnam 1993:177)

One does not have to repeat Putnam's hyperbole in black and white to see his point. His emphasis on trust may again invite the "unitarian" idea that the vitality of citizenship could be restored by efforts to reestablish trust. However, this would fly in the face of Putnam's observation that trust is an emerging property of voluntary ways of dealing with differences. It arises out of antagonistic cooperation—or in terms of this book, out of the organization of plurality by citizens.

The resilience of civil society lies in its capacity for self-organization, in its diversity of real life experiences and its capacity to learn from and to organize them. Learning from one's own and other people's mistakes *and* successes. Learning through variety and selection. When the government with its exclusive authority and its massive resources of knowledge gets too close or becomes too overpowering, such learning is stifled by attempts to learn by way of (the best) analysis and instruction, which is characteristic of monopolistic organizations and unitary structures. Therefore, the state should keep its distance from civil society if it wants to drink from this source. However, too much distance is also wrong. Then people will no longer be interested in politics and will use public provisions in a selfish and purely calculating manner. How can one know the right distance between government and civil society? Neither theories of government nor those of civil society give much help here. They refer us back to where we started: to citizens' own judgment.

Thus, in our search for sources of citizenship, we again and again arrive at where we started: citizenship itself. This is so because active citizenship is an important ingredient of such sources. "A conception of one's role and obligations as a citizen, coupled with a commitment to political equality, is the cultural cement of the civic community" (Putnam 1993:183).

So we have come full circle in this chapter. We asked about the vitality of citizenship, and about sociomoral conditions that are conducive to it. Following the trail of politicians who called on citizens to show more civic responsibility, intellectuals who argue for a new nationalism, and Putnam, who sings the praise of civil society, time and again we have arrived at our point of departure. It turns out that the most important factor making for the vitality of citizenship is the reproduction of citizens in the political process itself. Not through indoctrination and training in political correctness but by organizing differences in such a way that they, as a by-product, stimulate trust and enable people to learn and experience what it takes to be a citizen. In law courts, in activities in political parties, debates in mass media, and above all in the fulfillment of public offices.

I conclude: First, little is known and much remains uncertain about the sources of vital citizenship. Second, those social configurations that we know to be related to vital citizenship can be fostered and protected, but cannot be brought about through social engineering and moral appeals. Third, the best way to foster and feed those sources is to exercise citizenship.

To avoid misunderstanding, I want to emphasize that although this chapter has criticized unitarian moralizing, by no means do I wish to belittle feelings of nationalism and civic responsibility. People are free to feel proud of their nations; but such feelings are not obligatory for all. Those who lack or reject national pride do not thereby cease to be good citizens. In the same token, one might rightly insist on the legitimacy of one's own sense of moral responsibility, but such a responsibility is neither an obligation of all citizens nor a requirement for good citizenship.

ELEVEN

□ □ □

Political Institutions and the Idea of Citizenship

Political institutions are eminently important for the formation of citizens. They tell them what they may do, offering a repertoire of actions, and they provide them with rights they can use as trumps against other actors and institutions. They also feed an idea of what citizenship is and could ideally become. The ensemble of public institutions that we call a liberal democratic constitution is ordered with a view to making the voice of the citizen count. Without democratic institutions that give the individual voice a place in an order of voices and decisions, citizenship cannot be exercised and reproduced in action.

Institutions of liberal democracy are well known and analyzed (an excellent recent treatment is Holmes 1995). The issues they regulate include: the vote; accountability of rulers and the right to dismiss them; lawmaking and setting the major lines of public policies; free speech and rights of demonstration, assembly, and association; access to information and to media; and limitations on the use of money and violence in politics. Institutional forms differ across regimes, but there is agreement that if regimes are to be called liberal democracies, they need to address these issues in such a way as to secure citizens an effective voice in the public hierarchy. The point of these institutional arrangements of liberal democracies, one could say, is the freedom of citizens.

Before 1989, liberal ideas of justice and the institutional practices of liberal democracy to a large extent determined the contours and content of citizenship. Nowadays, this tight connection no longer holds. The idea that there is one theory of justice that can be put to work in all situations in the public realm has been discredited. Many now consider notions of justice to be plural and local. And the institutions of liberal democracy are often out of joint: They no longer function as harmoniously as they used to. Instead of citizenship and democracy working in tandem, we now hear political elites complaining that democracy is overburdened by overly active and demanding citizens. There is widespread concern about the gap between politics and ordinary citizens, but also fear that bringing them closer together, for instance through a referendum, will only increase mistrust. There are widespread doubts not only about the present functioning of existing liberal democratic institutions but also about the viability of liberal democracy as a program for constitutional construction and reform.

Established liberal democratic institutions may be criticized, but because they are supported by cultural routines and expectations, they continue to function, however imperfectly. In newly established democracies such as those in eastern Europe, and in new political regimes, such as the European Union, that are not nation-states, things are more difficult. There, liberal democratic ideas must be translated into a constitutional design for institutional practices, which in turn, it is hoped, will generate the supporting political culture that democratic institutions need to keep functioning. When institutional practices do not get off the ground to begin with, the routines and expectations of a liberal political culture cannot develop.

EUROPEAN CITIZENSHIP

The fate of democracy and citizenship in the European Union offer a telling example. For a long time, European institutions developed without adequate democratic controls. There was no parliament and no other democratic device that enabled citizens to effectuate a change of rulers. When direct elections to the European parliament were finally held, voter turnout was low. Parties at a European level did not really develop. What went under the name of parties were loose federations of like-minded national parties. In the European parliament there were quite a number of absentee members who only showed up when some bold action by the parliament had to be stopped. The parliament never voted European governing elites out of office. Many observers, like those at the authoritative weekly *The Economist*, have given up on the European parliament. They think that it will never succeed in making good the European democratic deficit. If democracy is to be realized at a European level, they think it will certainly not be along lines that copy the institutions of national parliamentary party democracies.

The question of citizenship was addressed by the European Council held at Fontainebleau in 1984. A year later, the Adonnino report (Commission of the European Communities 1985) proposed a step-by-step approach: first, symbols such as a flag and a European hymn (a theme from Beethoven's Ninth Symphony); then education through information and exchange of teachers and pupils. After such measures of cultural integration had begun to take hold, further small steps could be taken toward effective European citizenship, such as the granting of voting rights in local elections to all European Union citizens. For most people, however, European citizenship has remained stuck at the symbolic level or is simply irrelevant, because whatever European citizenship exists remains unconnected to effective control of real policy issues. The Maastricht treaty instituted a European citizenship; but like the other parts of the treaty, these clauses have not come alive in the hearts of the new Europeans. Nor has the treaty led to any deepening of legal, socioeconomic, and political citizenship at the European level. On the contrary, the institution of second and third pillars (for matters of justice and foreign policy) of the European Union has kept matters outside the legal controls that have restrained policymakers in matters falling under the traditional first pillar. All in all, European citizenship remains mired in the cultural sphere, without real legal and political incisiveness. Small wonder, then, that many people remain uninterested.

REDEMOCRATIZATION

It is not only in new polities like those of the European Union or in newly liberated regimes like Romania's that democratic institutions are in difficulty. This is also the case in established democracies, where calls for "redemocratization," for constitutional reform, and for citizen referenda are the order of the day. These states are having difficulty coping with extreme right-wing parties (for example, the Front National in France); with regionalism; with footloose firms in the globalizing economy; and with citizens who have lost interest in politics at the level of parties in the nation-state. Have liberal democratic institutions lost their power to generate enthusiasm and renewal?

Such failures of liberal democracy as a program of constitutional construction and reform may be avoidable. Maybe it is possible to realize the idea of a republic governed by citizens by a means other than that of party-parliamentary democracy. Citizenship may serve as a compass for keeping constitutional politics on course toward an unknown future. What the outcome will be, no one yet knows. It is clear, however, that if it is to be called a republic, citizens will have to play a crucial role as actors and as a guiding value in its new constitution. Citizenship, then, works as a value around which new choices and institutional arrangements can form and cluster. Citizenship is more than an established institutional reality; it is also an idea that is critical of existing institutions and that gives institutional reform its direction. This chapter illustrates this role of citizenship in the reconstruction of liberal democratic institutions from four perspectives: the public sphere, representation, loyalty, and freedom.

THE DIALECTIC OF PUBLIC AND PRIVATE SPHERES

The terms "public" and "private" refer to spheres of activities: A house is private; the street is public. Physical location, however, is not the decisive factor. The question is how people place their activities and keep them separate. Something that is appropriate in one sphere is often prohibited in the other. Public and private spheres have different rules for admission, for internal interaction, for holding people responsible, and for exit. A public sphere is accessible to anyone who can be regarded as a member of the public. This general accessibility is guaranteed by the constitution and other laws. Access to private spheres is also regulated by law, but a subjective element is central in these arrangements: the decision of the "owner" of the sphere about admission to it. The boundaries between the public and the private spheres are guarded. Unauthorized and irregular crossing of these boundaries is experienced as annoying, improper, offensive, or corrupt. It is primarily the citizen who is authorized to cross the border in both directions. Crossings by other actors are allowed only so long as they respect and serve, directly or indirectly, this authority of the citizen.

The existence of both a public and a private sphere is crucially important for freedom. Someone who is caught in one sphere and is at the mercy of the logic and power relations of that sphere, is not free. Freedom requires the possibility to say no, to refuse, to distance oneself. Without a sanctuary in which one is safe and cannot be punished for the critical attitude one adopts, this cannot easily be conceived. Freedom and critical awareness presume an eccentric position, an "I" from the viewpoint of which the relationship between the self and the world can be considered. An eccentric position regarding the exercise of public power requires a worldly anchorage—in weapons, a home ("my home is my castle"), or a private sphere protected by law. An eccentric position with regard to the exercise of private power (for instance, violence in the home) also requires a worldly anchorage—in public spaces, police assistance, freedom of association and meeting, freedom of the press, and the right to vote.

In the eighteenth and nineteenth centuries, the idea of a (civil) society was developed in the work of the founding philosophers of the Scottish Enlightenment, Hume and Smith, and of the "grand" theorists Hegel and Marx. It explained the logic of a sphere of practice in which people, within certain limits, look after their own interests. Which values and atti-

tudes and which collective outcomes that have not been consciously chosen by any of the participants does this process of interest articulation entail? The new sciences of sociology and economics addressed this issue. In
spite of all their differences, scholars from these fields agreed on the following: The possibilities for effective political action depend on (the insight into) processes in society.

This was also held to be true for citizenship. Insofar as it situated itself
outside the boundaries of what the dynamics of society allowed, it would
remain an illusion. Citizenship and freedom could only be promoted by
riding the most favorable currents within the dynamics of a society.
Some—for example, Adam Smith—were more optimistic about the possibilities of doing this than were others—Karl Marx, for instance. Yet none
harbored the facile thought, which later became popular for awhile, that
society would automatically render the correct civil attitudes; that upbringing in family, church, and school and the pursuit of one's own interest would quasi-automatically generate good citizens.

Anyway, it is clear that in our time the free interaction of social forces often does not spontaneously produce good citizens. We observe "free rider"
behavior, a plurality of normative orientations, and an increasingly international orientation that bypasses the framework of the nation-state. Relations between the economy, the family, and the church and their importance for the public sphere are disputed and no longer taken for granted.
Also, we no longer succeed, from within the public sphere, in mapping the
dynamics of the private sphere with a view to intervening in such a way
that citizenship is generated. More than before, therefore, citizenship now
has to be reproduced and guaranteed primarily in the public sphere itself.

Over the last twenty years, several West European countries have witnessed a drive toward narrower boundaries of the public sphere and toward stronger government within these limits. Its key elements have
been privatization of state activities, restriction of government to its core
tasks, and restructuring of the welfare state. The pursuit of socioeconomic
equality no longer takes a central place on the political agenda. This does
not imply, however, that civic equality within the public sphere has become unimportant. It remains of crucial importance for the reinforcement
of the public sphere within its more confined boundaries. This reinforcement also entails that the government may take corrective action outside
the public sphere insofar as this is necessary for the realization of actual
equality of citizens within the public sphere: no slavery (with a view to
freedom), no starvation (with a view to living); an open society (so that
independent formation of judgment remains possible); and reasonable
chances for newcomers, such as children and immigrants (so that their
obtaining property and other matters that provide security and satisfaction remains possible).

The terms "public" and "private" do not always stand for the same spheres. It is usually clear from the context what is meant. Roughly, there are three spheres at issue, the public-political, the public-social, and the personal-private sphere (Castoriadis 1997:7). The first one is that of political and administrative decisionmaking about the (adjustment of the) organization of society. The second sphere relates to the interaction between people, legal as well as natural persons, in (semi)public places, such as the street. The third sphere is that of home, friends, and associations. Three spheres and two words (public and private) can lead to confusion. The second sphere is sometimes regarded as private—as with "privatization"—and sometimes as public—as with "making private matters public." This ambiguity can be observed also in the use of the word "citizen." Sometimes this refers to participation in political decisionmaking (*citoyen*), and sometimes to participation in social interaction (*bourgeois*, the "ordinary" citizen versus the government). This usage causes more confusion in theory than it does in practice.

However, what does become clear from these considerations is that the term "private sphere" is itself ambiguous and requires further specification in practical usage. It may refer to a multinational firm like Shell and to a welfare mother, to a home and to the city park, to the church and to the business firm. Equating the private sphere with the market, with the pursuit of personal interest, with brotherly care, or with business is therefore inaccurate, or rhetorical trickery. Mutatis mutandis, the same goes for a further unspecified use of the term "to privatize."

The boundaries between public and private thus turn out to be historically and situationally variable. This does not pose too many problems in practice. These boundaries are man-made, a cultural artifact. However, the requirement that in order to be free, people must have access to at least two different spheres holds across the variety of cultural artifacts. In the republic, the private should be protected when it is at risk of being overwhelmed by public demands and considerations; and conversely, the public should be saved from being submerged in the private. Public as well as private places should remain intact and accessible to citizens. An overriding claim of either sphere over the other is fundamentally wrong.

REPRESENTATION

Representing—in a sense, making present what is absent—occurs often in daily life. A map, a bees' dance, and a report all represent how matters stand. We can often verify whether, or experience painfully that, a certain representation was incorrect. The world was not as it was represented; the representation proved unreliable.

Representation of people entails speaking and acting in behalf of others. These others are usually absent, but this need not be so. A chairman at a meeting speaks on behalf of the people present, and a lawyer represents a client who may also be present. Verification of the correctness of the representation of people has its peculiar aspects. After all, it is not the representation of established facts or things that is the issue here. What is represented is the speaking and acting of the person represented—not an object, but his will, his person. How can one establish that the representation is incorrect? The will, which is a notoriously subjective element that is moreover bound to change with time, has to be the decisive factor in this. Things become even more problematic when representation involves a large number of people, each with his or her own "will." And yet, here too, one can continue to speak of representation only so long as its verification remains possible. After all, it is absurd to speak of representation when the claim that someone or something is represented can never be verified.

Representation of people can be tested in various ways. The representation can be willed and authorized in advance. The representative may have said or done exactly what the represented person wanted to do or say. Or represented persons can confirm their trust in the representative even if they, had they been present, would have willed and acted differently.

Rousseau rejected political representation because, according to him, the will cannot be represented. Yet, in contemporary republics, in which direct democracy is not possible, some form of representation is indispensable. In a representative democracy, citizens holding offices represent those who are absent. Such a democracy has procedures for answering the following questions: Are the absentees truly represented (is the representation correct?); who is to determine this; and how and when does correction of failing representation take place?

When searching for answers to these questions, neorepublicans use a variety of theories of representation (Pitkin 1972)—representation as symbolization, as being formally authorized (as in Hobbes), as portrayal, as possibly being called to account, and as substantive promotion of interests. We can easily find circumstances in which each of these theories or visions obviously makes sense. However, are we not inconsistent in accepting this variety of theories? Should we not choose? Many discussions seem to assume as much. They assume that it is necessary and possible to use one and only one theory of representation in the public sphere. But why? The judge is representative in a way quite different from the member of the city council. The drive toward one single conception is, it seems, fed by a longing for an ideal, guaranteed system of representation. But no such guaranteed system can exist. Searching for it, however, is understandable. After all, representation presupposes a gap, a distance between the represented and the representative. At the same time, it assumes the duty and pretension to bridge this gap. However, if efforts to bridge the gap were guaranteed to succeed, then there would be no reason for representation. Representation by its very nature can never be a guaranteed success. We can deal with the gap between the voters and the elected in different ways, some of them bad, some better, but we can never eliminate it.

This applies even more in our time, when society is much less neatly organized and controllable than in earlier days. In contemporary society, established systems of representation will have to be adjusted and supplemented in an ad hoc way, time and again. Permanently fixing such supplements is not very useful, because there is a ready chance that the next time, other supplements will be needed. Representation becomes more tailored to each case, and a repertoire of various institutions and theories is used for this purpose. The search for one system that guarantees success is given up. Instead, we try to enrich our repertoire of institutions and theories of representation, to sharpen its tools and to make them mutually compatible so that they can be connected (in series, parallel, or in a political "story" or constitution).

Representation implies room for correction. Does this mean that we may conclude from the correction of representation that this representation was not right, not correct? No, not always. What is required to keep endorsing representation is not its correctness in each case, but its overall reliability. A correction every now and again can make representation more reliable. Without room for correction, the trust put in the representation cannot be tested. Without it, we cannot decide whether we want to continue putting our trust in the representative. When there is no trust, there is no representation. Representation is not a matter of precise portrayal but of giving and withholding trust. If a vote of confidence cannot be asked for at set times, true representation cannot exist.

Individual citizens are central in matters of representation—not just "ordinary" citizens but also citizens as holders of particular public offices such as member of parliament, judge, soldier, and policymaker. As citizens, they judge whether a vote of confidence should be asked for and they start procedures to correctly carry out such a vote. As citizens, they have a certain degree of immunity, a status that provides them the room to do this. Where this citizens' perspective is lacking, there is no democratic representation. A republic is not a direct democracy, but it is shot through with direct citizenship.

LOYALTY

Loyalty suggests having a home, one's own place in familiar surroundings of people and objects. It suggests ties that are not based on calculation but that, on a deeper level, form a basis of the values that enter into calculations. Loyalty exists in relation to places, people, and ways of act- ing—in relation to king, nobility, peers, workers of all countries, village, city, nation, and religion (cobelievers); and since recently, people of the same sex, animals, and nature. The quality of the connection we call loy- alty may differ: Loyalty can be absolute or limited, slavish or indepen- dent, open and relativizing or reticent and intolerant, obtuse or intelli- gent. Loyalty has the beauty of elementary dedication (such as that of the mother toward the child in the story of King Solomon and the switched babies [I Kings 3:16–28]), allegiance, and purity, but it also has the ugli- ness of exclusion, lack of freedom, and the closed society. The transition to an open society—which was at issue in the various renaissances, in the Enlightenment, and in movements for modernization and political eman- cipation—meant a liberation from established loyalties. (Other loyalties often resulted from this liberation, which were different but often no less binding and "established" than the old ones.) In an open society, loyalties should not be a fixed given but should be freely chosen from a variety of options. Moreover, one should retain the option of disengaging oneself within a reasonable period of time from loyalties that one had chosen (or acquired) in the past. This means that an open society faces specific prob- lems of organization: How can the interaction between a plurality of loy- alties be arranged in such a way that these loyalties are respected and can be preserved, so that the one is not destroyed in the encounter with the other, and so that individuals can relatively freely move among the plu- rality of loyalties?

The republic arranges the interaction between the loyalties of its citi- zens. To be able to do this, the republic itself must be able to count on the loyalty of these citizens. Civic loyalty, then, concerns loyalty to the repub- lican ways of dealing with plurality. Formerly, the law was central here. Public virtues primarily concerned conduct with regard to making, en- forcing, and obeying the law. Making law central—no binding of citizens except by choice, or by law created in freedom by citizens—is and has al- ways been problematic. To guarantee the power of the law, more is needed than the law itself. Even Rousseau thought it necessary to call upon a visionary leader and civil religion to establish the authority of "the general will." Current attempts to revive such a civil religion have had little impact. Hegel, Durkheim, and other theorists of civil society and its modern division of labor thought that this society would generate its own morality and culture, which would then serve as a basis for ap- propriate legislation. Later, however, Bell (1976), Hirsch (1976), and oth- ers found that capitalist society undermines its own moral conditions of existence and does not automatically produce new ones. Foucault (1975) argued that the reality of law, rights, and duties could function only because of disciplinary practices that unfolded outside the reach of that legal reality. In our time, however, this kind of discipline in schools, prisons, and homes is no longer taken for granted and has lost much of its effectiveness. Rituals that used to confirm the authority of the law are now regarded with suspicion, if they occur at all. In The Netherlands, a pillarized but vital structure of voluntary associations used to be the key element of consociational democracy. It fulfilled a crucial role in the establishment and enforcement of the law. At present, the remnants of these consociational structures are to a large extent financially and procedurally kept alive by the state, while they no longer command the support and obedience of many citizens. They do not "grow" from civil society but are rooted in the state—in "ideological state apparatuses," as they were called in the 1970s.

In the nineteenth century and the first half of the twentieth, the nation was the most important and most common repository and guarantor of the authority of the law. The nation, this "large self" that appeared in a common past and a common future, was assumed to coincide with the state and with civil society. In fact, the state and its legislation played an important role in the creation (and destruction) of nations, not only outwardly but also within its boundaries. Military service; compulsory education; the use of one language; the building of museums; and the production of maps, population statistics, and surveys were all brought in to create the nation, this "imagined community" (Anderson 1991), to change "peasants into Frenchmen" (Weber 1976). Today, however, such a state approach to nation building is rarely viable. All sorts of nations and would-be nations create their own (would-be) state structures, underground or otherwise, and the citizens of internationally oriented societies do not want to be taught about nationalism by the state. Nationalism has not disappeared. On the contrary, it has recently grown stronger. But nationalism no longer lets itself be tempered, shaped, and incorporated by the state on behalf of the authority of the law. Nationalism now is a breaker rather than a supporter of the laws.

It turns out that nowadays one cannot find or found one single underlying loyalty that can guarantee the functioning of the republic and its laws. There is a shifting plurality of loyalties. In the midst of these, the citizens themselves must generate loyalty in their social interaction—loyalty to the community of citizens and to certain ways of dealing with plurality. They can no longer find it in the nation or in other coordinating belief systems and enthusiasms, but have to turn to the public sphere itself. There they try to generate dedication to certain ways of dealing with plurality openly and no longer secretly by means of the state-fabricated myth of an "existing" nation. The reproduction of citizenship—and hence of civic loyalty—is a task of the republic and therefore of the citizens themselves.

This loyalty is not the highest; it does not claim priority over other loyalties under all circumstances. It does, however, have a metafunction, a special position, in relation to other loyalties. But this implies no more than that civic loyalty "trumps" other loyalties under certain circumstances.

It follows from the above that in the admission to citizenship, factors such as descent, place of birth, place of residence, and place of work play a role as indicators of a connection, of loyalty to the republic, but that the connection with citizenship is the more important and decisive factor: the willingness and ability to be a citizen in this historically developed community, with its own language, parliament, and so on.

Does civic loyalty have to be so local and specific? Theoretically sound arguments can be provided to support this proposition. In any case, existing republics have marked local and specific characteristics. Each ensemble of institutions (ways of doing) that developed through evolution and that we call a republic is made up of historical "contingencies," and is path-dependent. The question is how to deal with these specific and unique historical traits in an internationalizing world. Should we promote them? Should we incorporate them in a growing international consensus, or common denominator (which may not be very large), or keep them apart? Neorepublicans will strive to retain this special character of their republic in a world community that has to rely on openness; but they will also try to make that character as compatible as possible with that of other republics. They also will attempt to keep transitions from one particular republic to another viable. A world language such as Esperanto does not work. A uniform system for republics of citizens does not work, either. A better prospect lies in networks of republics and their citizens.

In such a network, dual (or plural) citizenship, which was thought to be incompatible with the exclusiveness of the nation-state, is quite conceivable, even though its concrete organization requires creative thinking and meticulous care. Equally, the contrast between the particular and the global world culture need no longer be much of an issue. Within the network that we call world culture, various "creole" varieties develop—that is, various mixtures of the world-encompassing and the local. Neorepublicans deal with a diversity of loyalties and do not need one leader or one ultimate or basic ideology of the nation. This is not to say that living with a plurality of loyalties is a simple matter. In the execution of an office it often requires tragic choices, as it does in private life. Yet, neorepublican citizens no longer allow an ideology such as that of the nation to obscure these choices. Loyalty suggests having a home, one's own place within a familiar environment of people and objects. It suggests a connection that comes naturally and is not based on calculation. Loyalty is as indispensable as it used to be, but its content and reproduction processes have changed. The home of today's citizens is the public sphere in their repub-lic, and their familiar environment is the entire "creolizing," plural world. It is the world they watch on television, the products of which they can find in shops in the more prosperous countries, and the effects of which they notice in rich and poor countries.

In loyalty there are always elements of both the given and the chosen. When we want to know about loyalty, we immediately ask "loyalty to what or to whom?" The what and the whom are, we feel, both *given*, out there in the world, and *chosen*, opted for by the one who is loyal. Al-though the choice and the given are present in all notions of loyalty, there are sharp differences as to where they are to be located and how they are related. Many observers find the given basis of the loyalty of citizens in the nation, ethnicity, or culture. From a neorepublican perspective, this is taking the wrong given as a basis for choice and exclusion. The given is plurality, people who cannot avoid having to deal with each other. The point is to transform their relations in such a way that they can be ac-cepted by free citizens. This is not done by excluding some people and choosing others to relate with but rather by changing the relations be-tween given people in such a way that they are worthy of being cho-sen/accepted by citizens. This implies treating each of the people in-volved as much as possible as citizens. This does not require that citizenship be their safe and longstanding possession but rather implies treating them as "halfway" citizens, as citizens on the road to freedom, whose citizenship is in the making in their very interactions.

It is true that in order to transform the given of plurality into relations chosen by citizens, another "given" should be accepted: the laws and democratic procedures that make citizenship possible, that are constitu-tive of it. But these are a kind of second-order given that serves to trans-form givens of the first order. Such second-order givens should, more-over, not be made absolute, because they may be used self-referentially, that is, they themselves may be changed. In sum, neorepublican loyalty is loyalty to given plurality and to the ways it may be organized by citizens. Its point is to transform fate, or fortune, into an accepted republic of citi-zens. Freud wrote about treating chance as worthy of determining our fate. This is precisely what citizens do when they take chance, the given plurality of people who bump into each other, as the stuff that they feed their republic with.

FREEDOM

Just a few words on freedom. Not because the subject is not important, but because it is the heart of the matter. That makes it hard to talk about.

All institutions of liberal democracy point toward it, but when we try to tackle it directly, we hesitate and are easily dumbfounded.

Philosophers of law know that it is easier to indicate what is unjust than to grasp the essence of justice. By indicating and fighting injustices, they hope to encompass and approach justice, the great unknown. Yet they can never really grasp it. A similar *via negativa*, an approach by way of negations, is traveled in our search for freedom. Here, too, it is easier to notice the absence of freedom than to name and value its presence.

There is something strange in the appreciation of freedom. On the one hand, freedom is the core of liberal politics and ethics, the axiom on which all arguments elaborate. On the other hand, we know that freedom, sometimes, is not right for, or is not sought after by, free people. The enjoyment of freedom can break young people in their development or can make adults dig their own graves. Apart from this, various social-psychological experiments show that people who otherwise are quite normal and sane, in fact, in practical situations, often value freedom of choice negatively. Freedom is a key value the reproduction of which by free people is problematic. Citizens as such are supposed to pursue this value in their actions, yet people do not always act spontaneously as freedom-loving citizens.

Many descriptions of freedom exist. The well-known ones are negative freedom—no interference from others—and positive freedom—being able to realize what you want while taking into consideration the freedom of others. These can be summarized under the heading of personal freedom. In addition, two other meanings are distinguished: sovereign freedom—doing what you want even against the wishes of others; and civil freedom—participating in the life and the administration of the community of which you are a member (Patterson 1991:3–4).

As long as they remain static, these definitions and classifications do not enlighten much in times of constitutional change. A dynamic approach may work better. In the dynamic view, freedom is not a given, a kind of object, but something that appears in action, something toward which movement is directed. Freedom is something that appears, arises, and has to be understood in that movement. Citizens in action make freedom appear. When we observe their actions, we can reconstruct this movement from beginning to end. On the one hand, they act from a certain status, a position, of freedom; and on the other hand, the outcome of their citizen actions is an experience of freedom. When this initial status still has to be reached or is uncertain, we speak of liberation practices. When this status is taken as given and used as a matter of fact, we speak of freedom practices. This distinction involves no more than a difference in emphasis. Both aspects are always at issue to some extent. Freedom appears in the movement between the two.

From the requirements of minimal autonomy and competence, such that citizen action can begin to get going, it does not follow that citizenship is to be exclusively reserved for people who are fully free and competent. Such people do not exist at all. Nobody *is* free. Citizenship involves dealing competently with differences, dependencies, and unfreedoms. When people succeed in doing this, freedom appears. Freedom shows itself but is not a possession. When citizens succeed in doing this together, they generate power. This also is not a possession. Freedom, competence, and power appear in, and as by-products of, citizen action. Acting is beginning something new. Being able and having the courage to do this is a requirement of citizenship. This, however, is something else than a guarantee that the intended result will be achieved. Such a guarantee cannot be given by individual citizens, regardless of how learned, clever, and cunning they may be. The outcome is determined not so much by individual competence as by the acting together of a diversity of citizens, by the ways they find to organize their plurality.

The dynamic character of freedom was there from the start, when freedom emerged from the experience of slavery (Patterson 1991). Freedom appears in political history precisely at times of movement and unrest: in the Athenian "polis," the Italian city-states of the twelfth century, the Dutch republic of the Eighty Years' War. Freedom also appears in the way in which citizens fulfill special public offices. In earlier chapters I described how citizens generate freedom by dealing competently with plurality. The dynamic character of freedom emerged also in my discussion of public space, where I emphasized that the possibility of moving from one sphere to the other is an essential condition of freedom. The different spheres are governed by different rules, which allows people to use one sphere as a kind of sanctuary with regard to the other.

Citizenship can be conceived of as such a sanctuary in which people are free and equal. However, this static picture misses an important point, because the freedom at issue surfaces *in* the movement between citizenship and other areas of life. The relations of dependence that exist in these other areas are modulated by the sphere of citizenship. This does not imply the creation of equality in the social or personal spheres, but it does imply the adjustment of relations in such a way that access to citizenship is open to everyone. Such a modification of dependencies is not without problems.

The ban on slavery or recombinant forms of slavery is relatively undisputed, at least in theory. A slave is a person who is powerless in a relationship in which he is caught for a considerable period and which is dishonorable (Patterson 1982 and 1991). Citizenship and slavery are incompatible because slavery is the negation of the dual role of ruler/ruled.

Modifications of dependencies become more problematic when people who are not slaves apparently act in a constrained way—addicts, lunatics, or slavish followers of prevailing opinions and fashion. Intervention here is problematic, except when the dependency is permanent and obvious.

And what should one do with normal citizens whose formation of preferences occasionally but not permanently "misfires"? Their perception and evaluation may be formed in ways they would have rejected had they recognized them. Think of a fit of anger, of one-sided or incorrect information, and so on. Their choice is a free one, but it is not "purely," not entirely freely, brought about. Such problems arise regularly in the spheres of democracy, law, and education. The dangers of paternalistic compulsion or pressure and of unproductive accusations of "false consciousness" are considerable; but they cannot be prevented by announcing "freedom first" and then pretending all is well.

From a neorepublican point of view, it is clear which approach should be adhered to in situations of slavery or recombinants of slavery: emancipation, liberation practices, positive discrimination, and positive action. Yet the legitimation of such interventions ends where slavery stops. Farther-reaching elimination of disadvantages and the achievement of social equality are not requirements of neorepublican citizenship.

It is more difficult to determine an attitude toward the second and third sort of cases, the permanently addicted and the incidentally unfree. People who are free as well as unfree do not fit into the system of categories of citizenship. They are anomalies that need to be treated carefully. We want to retain the categories as well as secure the real freedom of the citizens, but these cannot be easily combined. Hence, we have complicated and circumspect policies concerning addiction to alcohol or drugs. And that is why we tread carefully when inaccuracies occur in the formation of preferences of citizens who are otherwise free. Such cautious interference with inaccuracies in the establishment of "free" judgments can be found in the practice of education, in contacts with people who sympathize with antidemocratic parties, and with lawyers who try to protect their clients from themselves by "urgently" advising them to do or not to do certain things. Neorepublican citizens acknowledge that such problems are inherent to a free society, to movement in which freedom surfaces. They realize that there are no standard solutions and therefore do not incessantly try to find them. They acknowledge the dilemmas of freedom and accept their responsibility for coping with them in ambiguous situations.

IN SEARCH OF PUBLIC CONTEXT

It is clear that the constitution of the public sphere, of the setting of institutions within which citizens can appear and act, is no longer self-evidently given. Some commentators complain that it has been taken over by the media, technical experts, market/price calculations, and established interest groups—in short, by actors and factors other than citizens debating and deciding among each other. Others do not subscribe to such pessimistic conclusions, but otherwise share the observation that the contours of public-political space are changing. This is most visible in the problematic role of political parties, which find it increasingly difficult to attract members and to organize public debate. The reconstitution of public-political space is on the agenda. How this new context for political action will look is as yet uncertain—multipolar, European, market-like, national parliamentarian?

Scarcity of context is a ubiquitous problem in our time. When information travels quickly and is abundant, the self-evident setting within which information acquires meaning and provides orientation may be lost. What is presently going on in politics is a struggle for the context of public action, a struggle about what will count as self-evident. What compass will guide us through this struggle? Will it be the nation, race, religion, or the traditional community? Or will it be civic dedication to the republic, to democratically and legally guided ways of organizing differences?

We have considered a few public institutions that are constitutive for citizenship in liberal democracies. We also have analyzed examples of how neorepublicanism can help us keep the politics of reform of those public institutions on course. This analysis of public institutions is far from exhaustive, but one thing is clear: In times of constitutional reform and turmoil, citizens are formed by the very struggles for reform that they engage in; by what is on their agenda; by what they do and fail to do. Citizenship is in the making. This is not a bad time for citizenship. Transition periods are risky, but they are also invigorating because they offer really good reasons for citizen action. As during World War II, something important is at stake. In such times, citizens can indeed make a difference.

The Outlook for Citizenship

Although many did not realize it at the time, 1989 was a watershed year, after which politics would no longer be the same. Political reform turned out to be more than a set of variations on established truths, themes, and principles: It became a journey into the unknown—a tentative groping in the dark, an exhilarating or bitterly disappointing common effort to invent new political forms and relationships, to reconstitute public space and viable forms of living together.

Although 1989 marked a liberation from oppression, it soon became painfully clear that this liberation was not identical with the triumph of liberal democratic ideas and practices or with the judicious implementation of a tried-and-true mix of market reform (privatization and competition) and democratization (parties and elections). Such "liberalization" often failed to liberate as was promised and hoped for.

And it was not only in new or restored democracies that the blessings of liberal reform failed to materialize. Established liberal democracies also were affected by the changes summarized under the label of "1989." Their trusted ways of conducting politics became undermined by criticism and disaffection, by internal splintering and external realignments. Externally, they were confronted with the end of the Cold War, with regroupings of nations, with new regimes and with nations splitting up, with the growing importance and reach of international organizations such as the European Union or the human rights court of justice in Strasbourg, with globalization and a worldwide economic boom. All this necessitated a repositioning of the sovereign national state. Was it still the major unit of action in the world? And if not, what would citizenship in a disempowered nation-state count for? Internally, established liberal democracies were confronted with increasing pluralization and difference; with groups that no longer considered the nation-state theirs; with nationalist separatism; and with citizens who showed no interest whatsoever in politics as usual.

These challenges, in turn, have led to the observation that politics has become decentered. The theme of the displacement of politics is echoed in one form or another in many contemporary writings. If it is indeed true that politics as usual is losing its center in political parties and parliaments in the nation-state, then the position of the citizen cannot remain unaffected. If those who are interested in the double position of ruling and being ruled turn to other arenas of political activity, then citizenship, in the traditional sense of participation in the institutions of liberal democracy, might evaporate into thin air. At the very least, its previously secure position of equality in the public realm is being transformed into an uncertain position in changing networks and processes.

There are good reasons to resist such a development. Although citizenship was meant to be for all, in networks there is little or no place for losers, for those who are not attractive enough to become a nodal point in such networks. Citizenship invited persons to act in a public space that allowed for difference, conflict, and nonnormal initiatives; but life in networks is much less friendly to what is not normal and what does not "sell."

Those who care for the values of citizenship and freedom for all therefore will not accept the displacement of politics as a simple fact of life. Where possible, they will oppose it or slow it down. And where it seems inevitable, they will try to realize the values of citizenship and freedom inside the new networks, in the places and relations to which what was known as politics has moved.

Some have accepted globalization as a fact and are working to realize the values of citizenship at a world level through human rights, humanitarian international interventions, a strengthening of world opinion, and alliances of democracies. Business leaders and multinational firms are urged to accept their responsibility to make this emerging world order a civilized one. A new order or new orders are surely in the making; but will they have enough bite to ensure the protection that citizenship in the nation-state used to provide? Whatever the answer may be, such a world order surely needs local allies and a firm anchoring in locally sovereign institutions.

This is emphasized by those who insist that the nation-state remains as indispensable for real citizenship as it was before. Citizenship needs a setting of authoritative institutions and culture if it is to make a real difference and to provide real protection. There is nothing in sight beyond the nation-state that can provide this. If the nation-state is in trouble, therefore, it needs to be strengthened by more, and more direct, political participation of ordinary citizens and/or by a more vigorous national culture. The first option, reinforcing the framework of the nation-state through more democracy, is eloquently advocated by Benjamin Barber (1995) in his study with the telling title of *Jihad vs. Mcworld*. The second option, relying on the local national culture and on feelings of belonging, is gaining popularity with an increasing number of intellectual commentators. In Chapter 10, I have given my arguments for rejecting that option.

Others insist that if citizenship is to make a difference, its place within the framework of the changing nation-state needs rethinking. They develop notions of deliberative democracy and agonistic models of politics that enable citizens to make better sense of the contemporary perplexities of democracy in nation-states (Benhabib 1996:9). These insights, both old and new, can then be used in other contexts—in regimes other than nation-states—where people bump into each other. Thus, Michael Walzer in an elegant study (1997) has applied, or rather, has sensitively "translated," insights on toleration that he has gained on his home ground to other regimes, such as multinational empires, international society, consociations, and immigrant societies.

This book has joined the rethinking of citizenship in its old and new settings. It is part of an ongoing reflection in political theory, which in turn is part of an ongoing politics of constitutional reconstruction. It shares themes and concerns with other studies, like pluralization in the work of Connolly (1995), or the insistence on nondomination in Pettit's study of republicanism (1997). Of course, it also differs from such studies. However, virtually all writers on the subject agree that after 1989, the nature of the political, and our understanding of the ideal role of citizens, cannot be taken for granted. Beyond that point, I cannot speak for them. Let me therefore, by way of summary of this study, speak for myself, and contrast my own theory of citizenship with contributions from before 1989.

Whereas the older approaches primarily analyzed the conditions that supposedly must be met before citizens can begin to act as such, neorepublicanism sees in the difficult and imperfect exercise of citizenship itself the main generative condition for the "reproduction of citizens." This stance has implications for the way we address questions of access, culture, and participation.

There cannot be citizenship if there is no *access* to it. Citizenship is not a natural attribute of people but a public status with specific conditions of access through education, immigration, and earning capacity or ownership. Ideally, in democracies, the status is accessible to all; but in fact, this is never the case. In order to make good the democratic ideal, many theorists previously focused on questions of access, of emancipation toward freedom rather than on its actual practice. Therein, they thought, lies the crucial test for any theory of citizenship. However, such demands overstretch theories of citizenship and tend to make them vacuous. A theory of citizen rights in migration, for instance, presupposes either a world-encompassing notion of justice or the realization of world citizenship. The real protection and exercise of citizenship, however, are ineluctably local.

Education for citizenship is an inherently ambiguous notion, because education requires and accepts inequalities that are inadmissible between full-fledged citizens. Theories that respond to people's hopes for the revitalization of citizenship through educational reform therefore are bound to disappoint. They try to restore citizenship by improving its conditions, by focusing on a setting of inequality and domination in which citizenship cannot be fully exercised.

We find a similar defect in approaches that squarely concentrate on improving the socioeconomic conditions of citizenship. Here, also, an emphasis on liberation, on freeing routes of access to citizenship, tends to overshadow the actual exercise of citizenship in practices of freedom. Obviously, the person who has nothing to eat and no place to sleep cannot survive and speak out as a citizen. But thinking about citizenship becomes a muddle if one makes socioeconomic security and social rights the crux of citizenship, as have the many followers of T. H. Marshall. The core of citizenship lies in the public realm, in acting as citizens, and not in the socioeconomic sphere of work. That people have no job or are unwilling to work may be unjust or morally wrong; but from the point of view of citizenship, these facts are only important insofar as they impinge on the individuals' performance as citizens in the public sphere.

Without *culture*, there can be no citizenship. However, from this it does not follow, as many have implicitly assumed, that a unity of values, virtues, or normative orientations is a requirement for viable citizenship. This study sees resilience and viable living together as arising out of the ongoing organization of differences. In order to be viable, a society of citizens needs, in the words of Albert Hirschman (1995:243), "a steady diet of conflicts." The cultural condition of citizenship is not consensus but a rich repertoire for acknowledging and dealing with conflicts. Consensus is not a condition but is the preferred outcome of organizing differences. True, if there never were some sort of consensus or peace between people, we could not speak of citizens living together; but an emphasis on consensus and cohesion through unity leads to wishful thinking. It posits the preferred outcome of interaction between citizens as its precondition. In this book, consensus is not considered a necessary condition for viable citizen action. Thus, my view differs from Rawlsian (Rawls 1993) notions of overlapping consensus; from communitarians like Sandel (1982), who emphasize the necessity of integration in a historical community; and from all those who put their hopes for a revival of citizenship on a strengthening of morality, virtues, and social cohesion. They all assume that a unity of feeling or convictions constitutes the cement of a republic of citizens. In contrast, in this book, I have focused on the irrational feelings, the hatred and the experience of difference that obtain between people who cannot avoid dealing with each other, people who find themselves connected in a community of fate. Such a community is given, not chosen. If the people involved act as citizens, they transform this community into a republic in which every person involved has the status of public chooser.

If no one actually *participates*, there is no citizenship. However, this study does not share the emphasis of many others on increasing participation. It rather focuses on those persons who, in whatever function and for whatever reason, are already active somewhere in the public sphere. How do their actions look from the point of view of citizens? Do these enhance or hinder the reproduction of citizenship? Do they remember and take into account what it is to be subjected to the power that their function entails? Do they know how to rule and to be ruled? The drive toward more participation and emancipation is laudable but tends to make studies exhortative instead of analytical. In its extreme form, it also self-destructs: The ordinary citizen is conceived of as powerless, and insofar as there is success in making him powerful in some specific sense, he ceases, by definition, to be an ordinary citizen. I fully agree with theorists who, like Benjamin Barber (1984), raise the flag of better public deliberation and participation by more citizens. The only difference is one of emphasis. Neorepublicanism expects to achieve the greatest effect from emphasizing the citizen qualities of ongoing participation in the public sphere, and therefore, does not focus exclusively on deliberative democratic processes but considers the exercise of citizenship in various other public functions, such as those of policeman, tax inspector, head of secret service, and press secretary. These public officers must cope with their differences with others as well as with differences within themselves, sometimes encountering tragic conflicts between the demands of special office and those of citizenship. Rather than focusing on the mobilization and instruction of complete newcomers, neorepublicanism focuses on improving and enlarging the repertoire and competence of those who, however clumsily, have already begun to participate. Citizenship is not a possession that may be achieved completely and secured forever but rather is constituted in its imperfect exercise by citizens, along the way.

References

Ackerman, Bruce. 1991. *We the People: Foundations*. Cambridge, Mass.: Harvard University Press.

———. 1992. *The Future of Liberal Revolution*. New Haven, Conn.: Yale University Press.

Anderson, Benedict. 1991. *Imagined Communities*. London: Verso.

Andrews, Geoff, ed. 1991. *Citizenship*. London: Lawrence & Wishart.

Arendt, Hannah. 1959. *The Human Condition*. Garden City, N.Y.: Doubleday Anchor.

———. 1965. *On Revolution*. New York: Viking Press.

———. 1968. *Between Past and Future*. New York: Viking Press.

Balibar, Étienne. 1997. *La crainte des masses: Politique et philosophie avant et après Marx*. Paris: Galilée.

Barber, Benjamin. 1984. *Strong Democracy: Participatory Politics for a New Age*. Berkeley: University of California Press.

———. 1988. *The Conquest of Politics: Liberal Philosophy in Democratic Times*. Princeton, N.J.: Princeton University Press.

———. 1995. *Jihad vs. Mcworld*. New York: Random House.

Bauböck, Rainer. 1994. *Transnational Citizenship: Membership and Rights in International Migration*. Aldershot, England: Edward Elgar.

Bell, Daniel. 1976. *The Cultural Contradictions of Capitalism*. New York: Basic Books.

Benhabib, Seyla, ed. 1996. *Democracy and Difference: Contesting the Boundaries of the Political*. Princeton, N.J.: Princeton University Press.

Brubaker, Rogers. 1992. *Citizenship and Nationhood in France and Germany*. Cambridge, Mass.: Harvard University Press.

Bruner, Jerome. 1990. *Acts of Meaning*. Cambridge, Mass.: Harvard University Press.

Burke, John. 1986. *Bureaucratic Responsibility*. Baltimore, Md.: Johns Hopkins University Press.

Castoriadis, Cornelius. 1997. "Democracy as Procedure and Democracy as Regime." *Constellations: An International Journal of Critical and Democratic Theory*. Vol. 4, no. 1 (April), pp.1–18.

Commission of the European Communities. 1985. "A People's Europe." *Bulletin of the European Communities*, Supplement 7–85. Luxembourg: Office for Official Publications of the European Communities.

Connolly, William. 1995. *The Ethos of Pluralization*. Minneapolis: University of Minnesota Press.

Dahl, Robert. 1956. *A Preface to Democratic Theory*. Chicago: University of Chicago Press.

———. 1989. *Democracy and Its Critics*. New Haven, Conn.: Yale University Press.

Dahrendorf, Ralf. 1988. *The Modern Social Conflict*. London: Weidenfeld and Nicolson.

De Haan, Ido. 1993. *Zelfbestuur en Staatsbeheer: Het Politieke Debat over Burgerschap en Rechtsstaat in de Twintigste Eeuw*. Amsterdam: Amsterdam University Press.

Den Hoed, Paul. 1992. "Ambtenaren als Burgers." Pp. 227–256 in *Burgerschap in Praktijken*, vol. 1, eds. Herman van Gunsteren and Paul den Hoed. The Hague: Sdu uitgeverij.

De Schaepdrijver, Sophie. 1995. "België als Kunstwerk, of de Versplintering van een Natiebegrip." *Beleid & Maatschappij*. No. 2, pp. 109–116.

De Winter, Micha. 1995. *Kinderen als Medeburgers: Kinder en Jeugdparticipatie als Maatschappelijk Opvoedingsperspectief*. Utrecht, The Netherlands: De Tijdstroom.

Docters van Leeuwen, Arthur. 1992. "Burgerschap in extremis." Pp. 245–259 in *Burgerschap in Praktijken*, vol. 2, eds. Herman van Gunsteren and Paul den Hoed. The Hague: Sdu uitgeverij.

Douglas, Mary. 1975. *Implicit Meanings*. London: Routledge.

———. 1987. *How Institutions Think*. Syracuse, N.Y.: Syracuse University Press.

———. 1992. *Risk and Blame*. London: Routledge.

———. 1996. *Thought Styles*. London: Sage.

Elster, Jon. 1983. *Sour Grapes: Studies in the Subversion of Rationality*. Cambridge: Cambridge University Press.

Etzioni, Amitai. 1988. *The Moral Dimension: Toward a New Economics*. New York: Free Press.

———. 1995. *The Spirit of Community: Rights, Reponsibilities, and the Communitarian Agenda*. London: Fontana Press.

———. 1996. *The New Golden Rule: Community and Morality in a Democratic Society*. New York: Basic Books.

Foucault, Michel. 1975. *Surveillir et punir*. Paris: Gallimard.

———. 1988. "The Ethic of Care for the Self as a Practice of Freedom: An Interview with Michel Foucault on January 20, 1984." In *The Final Foucault*, eds. James Bernauer and David Rasmussen. Cambridge, Mass.: MIT Press.

Geertz, Clifford. 1973. *The Interpretation of Cultures*. New York: Basic Books.

———. 1983. *Local Knowledge*. New York: Basic Books.

Gellner, Ernest. 1987. *Culture, Identity, and Politics*. Cambridge: Cambridge University Press.

Giddens, Anthony. 1994. *Beyond Left and Right: The Future of Radical Politics*. Cambridge, England: Polity Press.

Gould, Stephen. 1993. *Eight Little Piggies*. London: Jonathan Cape.

Gray, John. 1997. *Endgames: Questions in Late Modern Political Thought*. Cambridge, England: Polity Press.

Greider, William. 1992. *Who Will Tell the People: The Betrayal of American Democracy*. New York: Simon & Schuster.

Gutman, Amy. 1987. *Democratic Education*. Princeton, N.J.: Princeton University Press.

Gutman, Amy, and Dennis Thompson. 1996. *Democracy and Disagreement*. Cambridge, Mass.: Harvard University Press.

Habermas, Jürgen. 1981. *Theorie des kommunikativen Handelns*. Frankfurt am Main: Suhrkamp.

———. 1985. *Die neue Unübersichtlichkeit*. Frankfurt am Main: Suhrkamp.

———. 1992. *Faktizität und Geltung*. Frankfurt am Main: Suhrkamp.

———. 1996. *Die Einbeziehung des Anderen*. Frankfurt am Main: Suhrkamp.

Havel, Václav. 1987. *Living in Truth*. London: Faber & Faber.

———. 1992. "Paradise Lost." *The New York Review of Books*. April 9, pp. 6–8.

Heater, Derek. 1990. *Citizenship: The Civic Ideal in World History, Politics, and Education*. London: Longman.

Hirsch, Fred. 1976. *Social Limits to Growth*. London: Harvard University Press.

Hirsch Ballin, Ernst. 1992. *NRC Handelsblad*. February 27, p. 9.

Hirschman, Albert. 1970. *Exit, Voice, and Loyalty: Responses to Decline in Firms, Organizations, and States*. London: Harvard University Press.

———. 1982. *Shifting Involvements: Private Interest and Public Action*. Oxford: Martin Robertson.

———. 1995. *A Propensity to Self-Subversion*. Cambridge, Mass.: Harvard University Press.

Holmes, Stephen. 1993. *The Anatomy of Antiliberalism*. Chicago: University of Chicago Press.

———. 1995. *Passions and Constraints: On the Theory of Liberal Democracy*. Chicago: University of Chicago Press.

Honneth, Axel. 1994. *Kampf um Anerkennung*. Frankfurt am Main: Suhrkamp.

Ignatieff, Michael. 1993. *Blood and Belonging*. London: Chatto & Windus.

Iyengar, Shanto. 1991. *Is Anyone Responsible? How Television Frames Political Issues*. Chicago: University of Chicago Press.

Jordan, Bill. 1989. *The Common Good: Citizenship, Morality, and Self-Interest*. Oxford: Basil Blackwell.

Judt, Tony. 1994. "The New Old Nationalism." *New York Review of Books*. May 26.

Kaase, Max, and Kenneth Newton. 1995. *Beliefs in Government*. Oxford: Oxford University Press.

Karst, Kenneth. 1989. *Belonging to America: Equal Citizenship and the Constitution*. New Haven, Conn.: Yale University Press.

Kemmis, Daniel. 1990. *Community and the Politics of Place*. Norman: University of Oklahoma Press.

Kymlicka, Will. 1995. *Multicultural Citizenship*. Oxford, England: Clarendon Press.

Kymlicka, Will, and Wayne Norman. 1994. "Return of the Citizen: A Survey of Recent Work on Citizenship Theory." *Ethics*. No. 104 (January 1994), pp. 352–381.

Langman, M. A. 1992. "Arbeidsparticipatie is Vijgeblad voor Politiek." *Het Financieel Dagblad*. August 26.

Laslett, Peter. 1989. *A Fresh Map of Life: The Emergence of the Third Age*. London: Weidenfeld and Nicolson.

Lind, Michael. 1995. *The Next American Nation: The New Nationalism and the Fourth American Revolution*. New York: Free Press.

Linz, Juan, and Alfred Stepan. 1996. *Problems of Democratic Transition and Consolidation*. Baltimore, Md.: Johns Hopkins University Press.

Mandelstam, Nadezhda. 1974. *Hope Abandoned*. Tr. Max Hayward. New York: Athenaeum.

March, James, and Johan Olsen. 1989. *Rediscovering Institutions: The Organizational Basis of Politics*. New York: Free Press.

———. 1995. *Democratic Governance*. New York: Free Press.

Margalit, Avishai. 1996. *The Decent Society*. Cambridge, Mass.: Harvard University Press.

Marshall, Thurgood. 1950. *Citizenship and Social Class and Other Essays*. Cambridge: Cambridge University Press.

Mead, Lawrence. 1986. *Beyond Entitlement: The Social Obligations of Citizenship*. New York: Basic Books.

Meehan, Elizabeth. 1993. *Citizenship and the European Community*. London: Sage.

Milgram, Stanley. 1974. *Obedience to Authority: An Experimental View*. New York: Harper & Row.

Miller, Toby. 1993. *The Well-Tempered Self: Citizenship, Culture, and the Postmodern Subject*. Baltimore, Md.: Johns Hopkins University Press.

Moon, Donald. 1993. *Constructing Community: Moral Pluralism and Tragic Conflicts*. Princeton, N.J.: Princeton University Press.

Nicolet, Claude. 1976. *Le métier de citoyen dans la Rome républicaine*. Paris: Gallimard.

———. 1982. *L'idée républicaine en France: Essai d'histoire critique*. Paris: Gallimard.

Norton, David. 1991. *Democracy and Moral Development: A Politics of Virtue*. Berkeley: University of California Press.

Nussbaum, Martha. 1986. *The Fragility of Goodness: Luck and Ethics in Greek Tragedy and Philosophy*. Cambridge: Cambridge University Press.

Oldfield, Adrian. 1990. *Citizenship and Community: Civic Republicanism and the Modern World*. London: Routledge.

Pangle, Thomas. 1992. *The Ennobling of Democracy: The Challenge of the Postmodern Age*. Baltimore, Md.: Johns Hopkins University Press.

Parker, Julia. 1975. *Social Policy and Citizenship*. London: Macmillan.

Patterson, Orlando. 1982. *Slavery and Social Death: A Comparative Study*. Cambridge, Mass.: Harvard University Press.

———. 1991. *Freedom*. London: I. B. Tauris.

Peters, Tom. 1988. *Thriving on Chaos*. London: Macmillan.

Pettit, Philip. 1997. *Republicanism: A Theory of Freedom and Government*. Oxford, England: Clarendon Press.

Philipse, Herman. 1994. *NRC Handelsblad*. September 8.

Pitkin, Hanna. 1972. *The Concept of Representation*. Berkeley: University of California Press.

Polanyi, Michael. 1967. *The Tacit Dimension*. Garden City, N.Y.: Doubleday Anchor.

Przeworski, Adam. 1995. *Sustainable Democracy*. Cambridge: Cambridge University Press.

Putnam, Robert. 1993. *Making Democracy Work: Civic Traditions in Modern Italy.* Princeton, N.J.: Princeton University Press.

Rawls, John. 1993. *Political Liberalism.* New York: Columbia University Press.

Reich, Robert. 1991. *The Work of Nations: Preparing Ourselves for 21st-Century Capitalism.* London: Simon & Schuster.

Rescher, Nicholas. 1993. *Pluralism: Against the Demand for Consensus.* Oxford, England: Clarendon Press.

Roche, Maurice. 1992. *Rethinking Citizenship: Welfare, Ideology, and Change in Modern Society.* Cambridge, England: Polity Press.

Rorty, Richard. 1989. *Contingency, Irony, and Solidarity.* Cambridge: Cambridge University Press.

Rosas, Allan, and Esko Antola, eds. 1995. *A Citizens' Europe: In Search of a New Order.* London: Sage.

Ryle, Gilbert. 1963. *The Concept of Mind.* Harmondsworth, England: Penguin.

Sagan, Eli. 1991. *The Honey and the Hemlock: Democracy and Paranoia in Ancient Athens and Modern America.* New York: Basic Books.

Sandel, Michael. 1982. *Liberalism and the Limits of Justice.* Cambridge: Cambridge University Press.

———. 1996. *Democracy's Discontent: America in Search of a Public Philosophy.* Cambridge, Mass.: Harvard University Press.

Scheffer, Paul. 1995. "Nederland als een Open Deur." *NRC Handelsblad.* January 1.

Schnapper, Dominique. 1994. *La communauté des citoyens: Sur l'idée moderne de nation.* Paris: Gallimard.

Schön, Donald. 1987. *Educating the Reflective Practitioner.* New York: Basic Books.

Schuck, Peter, and Rogers Smith. 1985. *Citizenship Without Consent: Illegal Aliens in the American Polity.* New Haven, Conn.: Yale University Press.

Schwartz, Nancy. 1988. *The Blue Guitar: Political Representation and Community.* Chicago: University of Chicago Press.

Searle, John. 1996. *The Social Construction of Reality.* Harmondsworth, England: Penguin.

Shils, Edward. 1981. *Tradition.* London: Faber & Faber.

Sijes, Benjamin. 1974. *Studies over Jodenvervolging.* Assen, The Netherlands: Van Gorcum.

Soysal, Yasemin Nuhoglu. 1994. *Limits of Citizenship: Migrants and Postnational Membership in Europe.* Chicago: University of Chicago Press.

Sperber, Dan, and Deirdre Wilson. 1986. *Relevance: Communication and Cognition.* Oxford: Blackwell.

Spinner, Jeff. 1994. *The Boundaries of Citizenship: Race, Ethnicity, and Nationality in the Liberal State.* Baltimore, Md.: Johns Hopkins University Press.

Steiner, David. 1994. *Rethinking Democratic Education: The Politics of Reform.* Baltimore, Md.: Johns Hopkins University Press.

Sullivan, William. 1982. *Reconstructing Public Philosophy.* Berkeley: University of California Press.

Sunstein, Cass. 1996. *Legal Reasoning and Political Conflict.* Oxford: Oxford University Press.

't Hart, A. C. 1994. *Openbaar Ministerie en Rechtshandhaving.* Arnhem, The Netherlands: Gouda Quint.

Thompson, Dennis. 1987. *Political Ethics and Public Office.* Cambridge, Mass.: Harvard University Press.

Thompson, Michael, Richard Ellis, and Aaron Wildavsky. 1990. *Cultural Theory.* Boulder: Westview Press.

Toulmin, Stephen. 1992. *Cosmopolis: The Hidden Agenda of Modernity.* Chicago: University of Chicago Press.

Turner, Bryan. 1986. *Citizenship and Capitalism: The Debate over Reformism.* London: Allen & Unwin.

Turner, Bryan, ed. 1993. *Citizenship and Social Theory.* London: Sage.

Van der Ouderaa, ed. 1992. "Burgerschap en Belastingen." Pp. 41–98 in *Burgerschap in Praktijken,* vol. 2, eds. Herman van Gunsteren and Paul den Hoed. The Hague: Sdu uitgeverij.

Van Doorn, Jacques. 1992. "Burgers in Uniform: over de Relaties tussen Krijgsmacht en Staatsburgerschap." Pp. 195–212 in *Burgerschap in Praktijken,* vol. 1, eds. Herman van Gunsteren and Paul den Hoed. The Hague: Sdu uitgeverij.

Van Gunsteren, Herman. 1976. *The Quest for Control: A Critique of the Rational-Central-Rule Approach in Public Affairs.* London: Wiley.

———. 1991. "The Ethical Context of Bureaucracy and Performance Analysis." Pp. 309–325 in *The Public Sector: Challenge for Coordination and Learning,* ed. Franz-Xaver Kaufmann. Berlin: Walter de Gruyter.

———. 1994. *Culturen van Besturen.* Amsterdam: Boom.

Van Gunsteren, Herman, and Rudy Andeweg. 1994. *Het Grote Ongenoegen: over de Kloof tussen Burgers en Politiek.* Bloemendaal, The Netherlands: Aramith.

Van Gunsteren, Herman, and Paul den Hoed, eds. 1992. *Burgerschap in Praktijken.* 2 vols. The Hague: Sdu uitgeverij.

Van Gunsteren, Herman, and Edith van Ruyven, eds. 1995. *Bestuur in de Ongekende Samenleving.* The Hague: Sdu uitgeverij.

Van Steenbergen, Bart, ed. 1994. *The Condition of Citizenship.* London: Sage.

Vernon, Richard. 1986. *Citizenship and Order: Studies in French Political Thought.* Toronto: University of Toronto Press.

Viard, Jean, ed. 1996. *Aux sources du populisme nationaliste.* Paris: Éditions de l'Aube.

Vincent, Andrew, and Raymond Plant. 1984. *Philosophy, Politics, and Citizenship: The Life and Thought of the British Idealists.* Oxford: Basil Blackwell.

Walzer, Michael. 1994. *Thick and Thin: Moral Argument at Home and Abroad.* Notre Dame, Ind.: University of Notre Dame Press.

———. 1997. *On Toleration.* New Haven, Conn.: Yale University Press.

Ware, Alan. 1987. *Citizens, Parties, and the State.* Oxford, England: Polity Press.

Weber, Eugen. 1976. *Peasants into Frenchmen.* Stanford: Stanford University Press.

Weissberg, Robert. 1974. *Political Learning, Political Choice, and Democratic Citizenship.* Englewood Cliffs, N.J.: Prentice-Hall.

Wells, Charlotte. 1995. *Law and Citizenship in Early Modern France.* Baltimore, Md.: Johns Hopkins University Press.

Wiebe, Robert. 1995. *Self-Rule: A Cultural History of American Democracy.* Chicago: University of Chicago Press.

Wildavsky, Aaron. 1984. *The Nursing Father: Moses as a Political Leader*. Tuscaloosa: University of Alabama Press.

———. 1995. *But Is It True? A Citizen's Guide to Environmental Health and Safety Issues*. Cambridge, Mass.: Harvard University Press.

Wills, Gary. 1995. "The New Revolutionaries." *The New York Review of Books*. August 10, pp. 50–55.

Wittgenstein, Ludwig. 1958. *Philosophical Investigations*. New York: Macmillan.

Young, Iris Marion. 1990. *Justice and the Politics of Difference*. Princeton, N.J.: Princeton University Press.

Zinoviev, Alexander. 1981. *The Yawning Heights*. Harmondsworth, England: Penguin.

Index